Cooking with Apples

By Shirley Munson and Jo Nelson
with the Food Editors of Farm Journal

COUNTRYSIDE PRESS
a division of Farm Journal, Inc.
Philadelphia, Pennsylvania

ACKNOWLEDGMENTS

The authors wish to express their deep appreciation to Dr. Cecil Stushnoff, associate professor of Horticultural Science, University of Minnesota; to Leonard Hertz, associate professor of Horticultural Science and extension horticulturist, University of Minnesota, and to Ina Rowe, former extension nutritionist at the University of Minnesota for reading portions of the manuscript and giving valuable suggestions.

Some of the recipes in this book appeared in the *Minnesota Horticulturist* and are reprinted by permission.

Book Design: Michael Durning

Cover Design: Paul Panoc

Cover Photo: Ted Hoffman, Chas. P. Mills & Son

Library of Congress Catalog Card Number 75-18210

Contents

CHAPTER I

Apples in America

"The apple car is here! Hey, kids, hurry! The apple car just came!"

Screams of delight filled the air as the news spread among children shuffling home from school. Suddenly boys and girls were alive with energy, sprinting toward the railroad tracks.

In those days freight trains were commonplace in small towns of America and villagers looked forward to the crisp autumn day when the "freight" would pull a boxcar loaded with apples to a siding. As the door was pushed open, throngs of children were waiting to catch the red apples tossed to them. From town and farm, people came with gunny sacks and bushel baskets to stock up on apples, always a good buy from the apple car. Stored in a cool moist cellar, the apples would last most of the winter.

Often called "the king of fruits," the apple is probably the oldest fruit known to man. Many believe that apples were the forbidden fruit in the Garden of Eden. In the Old Testament, in Deuteronomy 32:10 and Psalms 17:8, both Moses and David used the expression, "the apple of his eye." Greek mythology tells of a golden apple inscribed "to the fairest" which actually caused the Trojan war.

Apple trees grew wild thousands of years ago in central and southwest Asia, China and the Near East. From there, the fruit was carried to Turkey, Israel and Europe. Charred remains of apples found in Stone Age lake dwellings in central Europe show that prehistoric man ate apples and dried them as well. When people began to cultivate crops, they planted seeds from wild apples in their gardens. At least 22 varieties were known to the Romans 2,000 years ago; when they invaded Britain, they brought along their apples.

In the Middle Ages, cultivation of apples (and other fruits) was taken over by the monasteries. The monks experimented with ways to make orchards more fruitful; their cultural methods became the foundation of apple orcharding.

Apples Come to America

By the time Columbus sailed West, apples were the most important cultivated fruit in Europe. The Spaniards who followed Columbus to the New World brought apples to Mexico and South America. The French carried them to the St. Lawrence River area in Canada. Years later, Spanish priests who founded missions in our Southwest planted apple seeds.

Crabapples were growing wild in North America but the fruits were bitter, sour and very small. In 1629, the Puritans of the Massachusettess Bay Colony planted apple seeds from England. The trees flourished in the cool climate, and from the time of the first settlements, apples have played an important role in American social history.

As the frontier moved westward, one man can be given more credit than any other for the hundreds of apple orchards that sprang up on the newly settled farms between the Allegheny and the Mississippi, and particularly in the Ohio River Valley: John Chapman— "Johnny Appleseed."

"Remember Johnny Appleseed,
All ye who love the apple;
He served his kind by Word and Deed,
In God's grand greenwood chapel."

—William Henry Venable, "Johnny Appleseed"

He has become a mythical figure, a hero of the folklore of the frontier, immortalized in song, story and poetry. The legendary picture is of a wiry man of medium height plodding along barefoot, wearing a coffee sack shirt, carrying a leather knapsack of apple seeds on his back. His saucepan hat doubled as a kettle in which to cook his mush.

The real John Chapman was born in 1774 in Leominster, Massachusetts, in September, appropriately—apple-picking time. Land records show that by the time he was 23—in expectation of a land rush to the area—he had selected a spot in beautiful virgin country in western Pennsylvania for his first apple planting. Until he died at the age of 71, he was obsessed with his passion for planting nurseries, moving them westward as the frontier was opening, always just ahead of the rush of settlers.

Every pioneer family hoped to have an orchard yielding fruit in as short a time as possible. As soon as they cleared some land and raised a cabin, an early task was to plant apple trees. An orchard was considered a sign of permanence as well as mastery of the land.

The problem at the time was to get trees. And that was where John Chapman—Johnny Appleseed—came in. He would visit the cider presses in the older, settled areas, wash out of the crushed apple pulp a bushel or two of seeds, pack them in his leather pouch and return to plant them on land he had bought or leased and cleared. After sowing the seeds, he would enclose the plot with a brush fence and spend some time cultivating his planting. Finally, he would put someone in charge to tend and later to sell his trees to new settlers. Then Johnny Appleseed would move on to another favorable spot with another pouch of seeds and go through the same operation.

Actually, there was nothing unusual about gathering seeds at cider presses and planting them in new clearings for future orchards. Many settlers did that. What was unusual about John Chapman was his larger plan of moving his apple seedling business westward with the frontier.

Forging into the wilderness, this Yankee tree peddler established a chain of plantings in western Pennsylvania, then across Ohio and into Indiana—always ahead of the big push of pioneers looking for good land. By the time settlers arrived, his seedling stock was ready to be sold or given away to those who could not afford to buy the trees.

Possibly his perseverance in establishing his trail of nurseries was connected with his missionary zeal for the Swedenborgian faith. As one of the earliest American converts to the Church of the New Jerusalem, it was his urgent desire to spread its doctrines. Besides his apple seeds, he carried with him as many of the publications of Emanuel Swedenborg as he could obtain. Whenever he could persuade anyone to read the books or tracts he carried, he would leave them until he came again. He would even divide the publications into parts, to make them go further, returning later with another section so they could be read in proper order. This unusual missionary actually started a kind of traveling library on the frontier!

Dressed in what looked like cast-off clothing, an animal skin or old hat on his head, his hair hanging down to his shoulders, usually barefooted, he was always the eccentric wanderer. He had no home of his own. He traveled back and forth on foot, horseback, by dugout or canoe to attend to his seedlings. He camped wherever he happened to be when night fell, or stopped at a cabin to ask for lodging. Usually he insisted on sleeping on the floor. He might read some of his Swedenborgian tracts to the elders or entertain the children with tales of his adventures in the wilderness with rattle-snakes, bears and wolves. He never carried a gun, for he had a deep respect for all living things. He died as he lived, looking after his plantings.

John Chapman's contribution in starting hundreds of apple orchards across the new frontier was probably not recognized by his peers in the early 1800's. But today, Johnny Appleseed is a hero. Bridges and highways have been named for him while apple festivals and plaques erected by historical and horticultural societies keep alive the myths and facts about this itinerant nurseryman. He identified himself as "by occupation a gatherer and planter of apple seeds." He has become a patron saint of orcharding and conservation.

Apples a Mainstay in Early America

To the early American pioneers, apples were a basic crop. No other fruit could be so easily started, and none was more versatile. The best apples were eaten fresh for dessert and made into pies and sauce. For later use, some of the fruit was peeled, sliced and hung in strings to dry from the rafters, or dried in the sun.

The French surveyor-farmer-explorer, St. John de Crèvecoeur, who settled on a farm in New York in late 1769, described how a great stage was erected outdoors on which apples were thinly spread to dry.

"They were soon covered with bees and wasps and sucking flies of the neighborhood," wrote Crèvecoeur. "This accelerates the operation of drying. Now and then they are turned. At night they are covered with blankets. If it is likely to rain, they are gathered and brought into the house. This is repeated until they are perfectly dried...

"It is astonishing to what small size they shrink," he went on. "The method of using them is this. We put a small handful in warm water overnight; next morning they are swelled to their former size; and when cooked either in pies or dumplings, it is difficult to discover whether they are fresh or not."

Apples Prized for Cider

The least choice apples from those early orchards were hauled to a nearby cider press and made into cider and vinegar.

Cider was the staple beverage in most households in Colonial America—barrels of it for the family to drink in early autumn when it was sweet and delicious. The early settlers had brought with them from the Old World their taste for cider as well as the knowledge of how to make it.

In the 1720's a village of 40 families is said to have made 3,000 barrels of cider. "Cider was, next to water, the most abundant and the cheapest fluid to be had in New Hampshire, while I lived there," wrote Horace Greeley, "often selling for a dollar a barrel. In many a family of six or eight persons, a barrel tapped on Saturday barely lasted a full week. . ." Since milk was considered a hazard for drinking, cider was the national beverage at least through the first half of the nineteenth century.

The White House Cook Book, published in 1887, gave a variety of suggestions on how to keep cider. Among them was this recipe:

"To keep cider sweet, allow it to work until it has reached the state most desirable to the taste, and then add one and a half tumblers of grated horse-radish to each barrel, and shake up well. This arrests further fermentation. After remaining a few weeks, rack off and bung up closely in clean casks."

The early American housewife needed cider and vinegar as flavorings and preservatives for the winter store of pickles, preserves, apple butters and mincemeats.

Apples, cider and vinegar could all be used as barter, too, for supplies the family might need and even to pay education expenses for the children. A diary dated 1805 mentions payment of "one-half barrel of cider for Mary's schooling."

Frontiersmen enjoyed hard cider as a normal social drink, providing cheer at weddings and other community gatherings. Often men carried a jug of hard cider to the woods or fields to help ease the backbreaking labor of a long day. In the first years on the frontier, however, before apple trees were producing, corn whiskey was the only alcoholic drink that could be made locally to any large extent. But as apples became abundant, part of the apple juice produced was diverted to make the highly potent liquor called applejack—the American term for apple brandy—sometimes referred to as "the essence of lockjaw." The fermented apple juice contained from .5 percent to 8 percent alcohol.

The apple juice from modern cider mills, unless sold to a distiller to make brandy, is usually pasteurized or treated with preservatives to keep it from fermenting. The sweet cider you buy in the grocery store or at a fruit stand is really apple juice, not cider. Fermented apple juice is hard cider.

Apple Butter and Apple Pies

The Pennsylvania Dutch can take credit for introducing apple butter to the American cuisine. Women of the neighborhood got together to chat and exchange gossip at apple paring bees. The apples they prepared were stirred into boiling cider in huge outdoor kettles. When it cooked down, it was a rich, dark, thick spread spiced with cloves, cinnamon or sassafras. Relished by every family, it was often eaten with cottage cheese *(schmierkäse)* on slices of homemade bread. The Pennsylvania Dutch were also experts at drying apple slices, which they called *schnitz*, from the German word meaning "cut." The apples they dried in the oven or in the sun were used in pies and such other favorite dishes as *schnitz un knepp,* apples with dumplings.

A classic breakfast in Pennsylvania Dutch country consisted of fried apples, fried mush and sausages. For frying, they chose the tastiest apples from their orchards, and sprinkled them lightly with sugar and cinnamon before serving.

Apple pie had been popular in Britain; in New England it soon became not only the standard dessert, but often a breakfast staple in many homes. Served with cheese, of course. "Apple pie without cheese is like a kiss without a squeeze," the saying went. At Yale College, every supper served for more than a hundred years is said to have included apple pie.

As the frontier moved westward, pioneer women carried with them the know-how for making apple pie. For many of the immigrants, however, apple pie was a strange but appealing new dessert. In 1851 a Norwegian immigrant who had settled in Wisconsin wrote home describing a wonderful dish called *Pai,* made of berries combined with sugar and syrup. "I can tell you this is something that glides easily down your throat; they also make the same sort of *Pai* out of apples. . . with syrup added, and that is really the most superb."

The Reverend Henry Ward Beecher, famous nineteenth century clergyman, paid an eloquent tribute to apple pie, declaring it should be anointed with sugar, butter and spices to form a "glorious unity. . . the morsels of apple neither dissolved nor yet in original substance, but hanging as it were in a trance between the spirit and the flesh of applehood. . ."

The First Apple Tree in Vancouver

Apples reached the Pacific Northwest in the early nineteenth century, not across the plains and mountains, but by sea. At a banquet in London in the winter of 1826, friends gave the captain of a Hudson's Bay Company vessel some seeds of a "good luck" apple. Captain Simpson was about to set sail on the hazardous voyage around Cape Horn to the Pacific Northwest; his friends wanted him and his men to have a reminder of their native England when they reached the new land. The good luck held; and, as his friends wished, Simpson planted the seeds in the spring of 1827, in the frontier outpost, Fort Vancouver, Washington.

From that beginning, the Washington apple industry has grown to be first in the nation. And the state's first apple tree still stands in the busy city of Vancouver, bearing fruit each year!

Commercial plantings in Washington spread rapidly through the eastern and central part of the state after the first irrigation project was completed in 1889. In 1894 the first railroad car of fruit was shipped from Yakima. Now an average of 30,000 refrigerated railroad carloads plus several tens of thousands of special refrigerated trailer truck shipments move Washington apples to all parts of the United States each year.

In the U.S. production of close to 150 million bushels of apples each year, Washington ranks at the very top. It produces about a fifth of all the apples grown in the country. If you eliminate the apples that are processed, the state's share is even greater. It grows, packs and ships about 35 percent of all apples sold fresh. With 85,000 acres in apple orchards, it's little wonder that the state of Washington has been called the Apple Bowl of the World.

Washington, New York, Michigan, Pennsylvania, California and Virginia account for about 70 percent of the United States crop. In Canada, British Columbia, Ontario and Nova Scotia produce the most apples.

About two-thirds of the apples grown in North America are sold as fresh fruit. The rest are canned commercially as applesauce and sliced apples, dried, frozen or made into sweet juice, cider and vinegar.

CHAPTER II

How Well Do You Know Your Apple Varieties?

Apples belong to the Rose family. Have you ever noticed how apple blossoms resemble tiny wild roses?

At one time there were thousands of different apple varieties grown in this country, but most of these have now disappeared. Some succumbed to disease and insects, others were left to die out because they did not sell or store well. Some trees were cut down by temperance workers fighting the evils of cider and applejack. Of the varieties that still exist, only about 25 are grown extensively in the United States and Canada. Less than that number make up over 90 percent of all apples grown commercially, though there are many small plantings of other kinds. Some of the old varieties are now grown for their historical value in an experimental orchard established by the Worcester County Historical Society in Northgrafton, Massachusetts.

The wild apple, ancestor of our modern cultivated varieties, was small and often sour. Through the years, man selected the best fruit for eating from wild trees and used the seed from the better fruit for planting. In this way, the quality of apples gradually improved over the centuries.

Apples, however, are among the fruits whose seeds do not "breed true." New trees grown from seeds almost never produce fruit exactly like that of the parent. Hence most seedlings are worthless. But every so often one bears such superior fruit—better than that of its parent—that it is propagated as a new variety. In fact, many of the present important varieties originated as choice seedlings.

Trees for today's orchards are produced by budding or grafting. That means uniting parts of two plants so they grow as one. A *bud* or *scion*—a short piece of twig—from a superior tree is inserted into a young seedling tree. The scion forms the top of the new tree. The new tree will produce fruit exactly like that of the parent tree from which the scion or bud was taken. Today, instead of doing their own grafting or budding, growers usually buy trees from nurseries.

By budding or grafting onto certain kinds of stock, nurserymen can produce dwarf apple trees. They've become popular because they are easier to care for and easier to harvest. And they often start bearing fruit sooner than larger trees.

The art of grafting is very old; no one knows who first grafted a tree. Perhaps people developed the idea from seeing natural grafts in the woods, where a branch of one tree becomes wedged in the crotch of another. At any rate, by 800 B.C., the Greeks had already written about their grafting techniques. Johnny Appleseed, however, our itinerant pioneer nurseryman, stubbornly stuck to planting from seed, possibly because he was convinced that was what the good Lord intended.

Many of the land-grant colleges and universities in the United States have fruit breeding projects at experiment stations. They work to develop apples and other fruits especially adapted to the climate of that region. Thus scientific breeding has resulted in some fine apple varieties.

Delicious: America's favorite eating apple

The leading apple variety in the United States is Delicious. It's sometimes called Red Delicious to distinguish it from Golden Delicious, which holds the second place ranking in production.

The Delicious apple originated on the farm of Jesse Hiatt in Peru, Iowa, in the last half of the nineteenth century. The story goes that Mr. Hiatt had planted an apple tree named Bellflower. It did not live, but the seedling root sent up a sprout which he nursed into bearing in 1872.

Twenty-two years later, in 1894, the Stark Brothers Nursery in Louisiana, Missouri, invited exhibits of fruit from all over the world to their fruit fair. Intrigued by the offer of prizes for the best specimens of known and unknown varieties, Jesse Hiatt packed a barrel of apples from his tree and shipped it to the fair. When the president of the company, C. M. Stark, tasted one of the apples, he exclaimed, "My, that's delicious!" The apples won first prize, but Hiatt's name was lost in the handling.

Stark Brothers repeated the fair the following year and again Hiatt sent a barrel of apples. This time the tag bearing his name was not lost. Sensing that this apple would win consumer approval, the Starks purchased all rights from Jesse Hiatt to propagate it as a new variety. The following year they introduced the new apple into commercial production.

There are more Red Delicious apples sold in the United States than any other variety; most of them grown in Washington state. Washington has more than 2½ million Delicious trees.

The fruit of America's favorite eating apple can easily be recognized by its elongated shape, the five distinct knobs at the blossom end, its sweet flavor and aroma. It has been dubbed "the sheep nose apple" because some see a resemblance between the knobby end and the nose of a sheep.

Golden Delicious: second in popularity

Golden Delicious is the product of a chance seedling discovered on the Anderson Mullens farm in Clay County, West Virginia. It was probably the result of a cross between Grimes Golden and the Golden Reinette, also known as English Pippin. In 1914 Mullens sent some of the fruit, which he called Mullens' Yellow Seedling, to Stark Brothers Nursery. The nursery was looking for a variety to complement its Red Delicious apple and purchased the new seedling, naming the fruit Golden Delicious.

Because of their thin skins, Golden Delicious apples were often bruised by the time they reached markets after shipping. But improved methods of packing, new containers and special handling procedures have now eliminated most of the problems.

Other apple varieties from seedlings

The third most important apple variety in the United States—and the leading variety in Canada—is McIntosh, descended from a chance seedling found in 1796 on a pioneer farm in Ontario, Canada. The apple was named for John McIntosh, the farmer who transplanted the clump of young apple trees he discovered while clearing land. By 1830 only one of the transplanted trees had survived, but the family liked the fruit from it so well that McIntosh's son Allen propagated it for his nursery business by budding and grafting. The original tree bore fruit for more than a hundred years.

By 1900 the variety was well known throughout the Northeast. Today, McIntosh is the favorite apple in New England and New York state.

Other choice varieties that came from seedlings include Baldwin, discovered by a surveyor working near Lowell, Massachusetts, in the 1790's; Northern Spy, found in Bloomfield, New York, about 1800; and Wealthy, developed from a seedling in Minnesota.

Peter Gideon and the Wealthy apple

The experience of Peter Gideon in developing the Wealthy apple in Minnesota is an example of the discouragement, yet courageous persistence of some of the early fruit breeders. In 1853, Gideon had moved with his family from Clinton, Illinois, to Minnesota and in 1858 he took up a claim of 160 acres of land on Lake Minnetonka, near Minneapolis.

For 41 years he worked to develop fruits for Minnesota growers that could survive the rigorous climate. In his first experiments after coming to Minnesota, he planted 30 varieties of apple trees and other fruits, to which he added annually. At the end of 10 years, rugged Minnesota winters had killed all of them except one lone seedling of a Siberian crab.

Though discouraged, impoverished, and with a large family to support, Gideon was still determined to produce a high quality apple hardy in the northern United States. He used his last $8 to send to Maine for seeds and scions. Eventually his dogged tenaciousness paid off; by 1868 he had successfully developed the Wealthy apple from the seed of the Siberian crabapple. He named it for his wife, Wealth.

The Wealthy apple became fairly important to the apple growers of the Northwest and in 1874 the red-striped fruit appeared on the Minnesota Horticultural Society's list of varieties recommended for Minnesota planting. Of the 14 varieties suggested at that time for planting, only Wealthy and Duchess still remain on the recommended list.

In 1912 a tablet in memory of Peter Gideon was erected on land that was once his farmstead, where he grew the original Wealthy apple.

What Variety Should You Buy

Some apple varieties are best for eating fresh, others for pie, still others for sauce or for baking. Some of the varieties you particularly like may not be available in retail stores. Depending on where you live, you may be able to obtain them at orchard sales rooms or apple barns. One of the joys of autumn is to take your family for a ride into the country to an apple orchard, an apple barn or a roadside stand. At many orchards, now, you can have the fun of picking your own apples.

Still more fun for the family, plus a learning experience, is the rent-a-tree orchard. You can actually lease a tree, enjoy the blossoms, check on the crop as it grows and then harvest it. The owner does all the work on your tree up to harvest time, while you visit the orchard whenever you can to see what's being done. Your family gets a real education in fruit growing—and the final reward of picking your fruit. A new development, rent-a-tree orchards may be hard to find, but they are worth the search for any family interested.

Your family probably has definite likes when it comes to choosing an apple variety for eating fresh. While many apples are "all purpose," some varieties are better than others for pies, sauce and baking. The chart on pages 24-28 describes characteristics of the most commonly available apples that come onto the market in mid and late fall. You'll want to refer to it as a guide for trying new varieties—and to get full satisfaction from the apples you buy.

What about early apples? Almost all of the apples that mature in late summer and early fall are local varieties. They're not shipped to market; they don't store well. Mostly, they're your "backyard apples," or available locally in season at roadside stands.

Depending on where you live, you may recognize their names: Beacon (also called Early Delicious, Fenton, Miller Red), Crimson Beauty, Duchess (or Oldenburg), Early McIntosh (Rob Roy), Gravenstein, Lodi, Mantet, Melba, Oriole, Summer Champion, Summer Red, Tydeman's Red, Wealthy, William's Red and Yellow Transparent.

The most widely grown of these early apples are

Duchess and Wealthy. Duchess is too tart for fresh eating, but good for pies, sauce and freezing. Wealthy is an all-purpose apple, medium-tart.

Most of the early apples are best for fresh eating, salads, fruit cups and desserts. They are also suitable for pie and sauce, and for canning and freezing. Refrigerate them and use them (or preserve them) within 3 to 4 weeks—they do not store well.

Promising new varieties are coming on the market. They include:

Late summer/early fall: Julyred, McLemore, Paulared, Prima, Puritan, Quinte, Raritan, Red Baron, Scotia and Viking.

Mid fall: Blushing Golden, Chehalis, Criterian, Empire, Holly, Honeygold, Jonamac, Mollie's Delicious, Ozark Gold, Priscilla, Regent, Spigold, Virginiagold and Wayne.

Late fall: Mutsu and Prime Gold.

How to Judge Apple Quality

Here are the quality indicators to look for when you buy fresh apples:

• Bright, sparkling color for the variety you select. Good color indicates full flavor. Don't be turned off by russeting—rough reddish-brown skin on part of the apple; this will not affect eating quality or flavor.

• Firmness, which is also a sign of good condition. Apples should be reasonably free of bruises since they may indicate poor handling, overripeness or even the beginning of decay. But when you test firmness, don't pinch—or you'll be responsible for adding bruises.

• The U.S. grade label, another indication of quality. Always check grade label before you buy. The federal government has specified grade standards based on maturity, degree of ripeness, uniformity of size, color and absence of blemishes. Most states have either adopted these grade standards or have similar ones.

U.S. Extra fancy and U.S. Fancy are the top grades. U.S. No. 1 meets minimum grade standards.

If you buy apples in perforated polyethylene bags, you should find this information on the packaging: variety, weight, size of apple, U.S. grade. For example, if you were buying Jonathan apples, you might find printed on the bag: Jonathan apples, U.S. Fancy, 2½″ minimum, net wt. 48 oz. (3 lb.), washed.

How much to buy

Buying apples by the bushel or half-bushel is usually more economical than buying smaller amounts. But before you buy a large quantity, ask yourself: How soon will I use these apples? Do I have the proper place to store them?

Your guide is to buy what you can store properly or use without waste. Medium size apples—a little less than 3 inches in diameter—are usually the best buy.

Suppose you want enough apples so you can go on an apple pie baking binge, with enough fruit left over for the family's lunches and snacks. Here's a table to help you calculate how many apples you need or can use, whether you're buying by the bushel, by pounds, or by numbers of apples.

---

1 lb. apples = 2 large, 3 medium, or 4 to 5 small;
                or approximately 3 cups peeled,
                sliced or diced fruit.

2 lbs. apples = 6 to 8 medium-size;
                or enough for 1 (9″) pie.

1 bu. apples = 40 lbs. or about 120 medium-size;
                enough for about 20 (9″) pies,
                or 20 to 24 quarts applesauce
                or 30 to 36 quarts apple slices.

How to Store Apples for Longer Keeping

If you buy apples in a perforated polyethylene bag, keep them in that bag in the refrigerator. The perforations allow air to enter the bag so that apples—with their living cells—can breathe. If you buy them in bulk, store them in the hydrator or in a covered container in the refrigerator to maintain proper humidity and prevent them from absorbing other food odors.

Apples purchased by the bushel or half-bushel will keep best, of course, in a cool, humid cellar. Unfortunately, modern homes rarely have cool cellars. You're in luck, though, if you have a second refrigerator—perhaps in the basement—where you have room for them. The refrigerator is an ideal place to keep apples over a long period, provided they are in a well covered container; otherwise they will dry out very quickly. With no refrigerator space available, keep apples in as cool a place as possible and line the bushel basket (or box) with aluminum foil or polyethylene to help prevent moisture loss. To increase humidity, you might also place a small container of water among the apples or cover the basket or box with moist towels.

Regardless of the quantity of apples you buy, a cardinal rule is to handle them gently to avoid bruising.

Red apples, polished to a high gloss, make a handsome centerpiece. But don't keep apples in the fruit bowl for days at a time. Apples will soften as much in a day at room temperature as they will in 10 days at 32° F. Moreover, the dry air will draw moisture and the fruit will shrivel, lose flavor and develop tough skin. So, to keep apples crisp and of good eating quality, hustle them back into the refrigerator between the times you need a decorative bowl of fruit for centerpiece or snacking.

Not too many years ago, once winter was over, it was hard to find good, firm apples to buy. But greatly improved varieties which keep longer and modern technology have solved that problem. Now you'll have little trouble getting good apples the year round. Fruit to be held for winter or spring selling is put into refrigerated storage immediately after it is harvested. It is cooled rapidly to about 32° F. where it is held until it is marketed.

Apples keep even better in controlled atmosphere (CA) storage. After the fruit is picked, it is put into a refrigerated, airtight room where the oxygen level is reduced and the carbon dioxide increased. This "controlled atmosphere" slows the life processes of the fruit cells and helps keep the fruit from getting soft. Many of the varieties which reach the end of their marketable life in normal atmosphere storage by mid-January will still be harvest-fresh through early summer under controlled atmosphere. However, they must be used quickly when they come out from CA storage because they deteriorate rapidly.

Since CA storage extends the market season so long, more and more controlled atmosphere storage plants are springing up in apple-producing sections of the United States.

Thus we have improved varieties and refrigerated and controlled atmosphere storage to thank for stretching the apple season so we can keep munching crisp apples until green apple time comes around once more.

Know Your Apples

Mid-fall

Variety	Characteristics	Uses	Availability in U.S. and Canada
Cortland	Medium size, attractive red with white flesh, similar to McIntosh. Holds fresh color well in salad. Mild flavor.	All-purpose: salad, sauce, pie, baking, fresh eating and freezing.	East, Central.
Delicious (Red)	Medium size, striped to solid red. Rich, sweet and mellow. Distinguished by elongated shape and five knobs at blossom end.	A favorite for fresh eating and salads. Not recommended for pie or cooking.	West, East, Central, South. Most available of all apple varieties and most popular in U.S. Washington State is number one producer.
Golden Delicious	Medium size, attractive yellow. Flavor rich, tangy sweet. Similar in texture and shape to Red Delicious.	Fresh eating, salad, baking sauce. Excellent all-purpose apple.	West, East, Central, South. Second most popular variety in U.S.
Grimes Golden	Mild and sweet. Green-yellow to golden yellow.	Excellent for fresh eating, salad. Good cooking apple.	East, Central
Haralson	Medium size, attractive red, tart and juicy. Developed by University of Minnesota.	All-purpose: pie, sauce, fresh eating, baking, freezing. The favorite for caramel apples.	Central, East.

Variety	Characteristics	Uses	Availability in U.S. and Canada
Idared	Attractive solid red, mild, crisp, small core.	Fresh eating, sauce, pie, freezing.	West, East, Central.
Jonathan	Below medium size, solid bright red. Tart, tender, juicy. Sweet flavor when cooked.	All-purpose: fresh eating, salad, pie, sauce, freezing. A fall favorite.	West, East, Central, South. Usually off the market by December.
McIntosh	Medium size, nearly solid bright red. Rich flavor. High quality for eating, but soft when cooked.	Fresh eating, sauce, pie, baking, freezing. Tends to be mushy in pie.	East, Central, West, South Leading variety in Canada and third most important variety in U.S.
Northwestern Greening	Attractive green or yellow, large size, slightly tart.	Pie, sauce, freezing.	East, Central.
Rhode Island Greening	Small to medium size, green to yellow-green, mildly acid.	Sauce, pie.	East, Central
Spartan	McIntosh type. Firm flesh, crisp, juicy, mildly tart.	Fresh eating, salad, fruit cup.	East, Central, West.
Winter Banana (Maiden's Blush)	Firm flesh. Golden Delicious type.	All-purpose: fresh eating, salad, pie, sauce.	East.

Late fall

Variety	Characteristics	Uses	Availability in U.S. and Canada
Baldwin	Dull red, mild flavor, firm texture	Fresh eating, pie, sauce	East
Ben Davis	Striped medium-red, medium to large size, mildly tart	Sauce, pie	East
Black Twig (Paragon)	Medium dull red, medium to large size, mildly tart	Fresh eating, pie, sauce, freezing	East
Connell Red	Solid bright red, medium to large size, sweet, juicy apple for fresh eating	Fresh eating, salad, baking	Central, East
Fireside	Large size, attractive red, rich, sweet flavor	Fresh eating, salad, baking	Central
Northern Spy	Large, striped red, tender, crisp and juicy with spicy flavor	All-purpose: fresh eating, pie, sauce, baking, salad	East, Central
Rome Beauty	Red with red stripes, shallow cup around stem. Firm, medium-tart to sweet	Best for baking and cooking, also for salad. Holds it shape in baking because of thick skin	East, West, South

Variety	Characteristics	Uses	Availability in U.S. and Canada
Stayman	Deep purplish-red, sometimes russeted. Rich flavor, moderately juicy	All-purpose: fresh eating, salad, sauce, pie	East, South
Winesap	Deep, purplish red, winelike flavor, tangy, firm, crisp, very juicy	All-purpose: fresh eating, salad, pie, sauce, baking	West, East, Central, South
Yellow Newton	Greenish-gold, delicately tart, firm, crisp, juicy. Good keeping apple	Fresh eating, pie, sauce, baking	West
York Imperial	Green, lopsided shape, mildly tart, firm, excellent texture, creamy yellow color when cooked	Sauce, baking, pie, fresh eating, salad	South, East. Limited fresh distribution because of demand for commercial processing

Crabapples*

Variety	Characteristics	Uses	Season
Centennial	Large, red-striped, yellow flesh, crisp, tender, juicy	Fresh eating, sauce	Late summer, early fall
Chestnut	Large, crisp, juicy, spicy flavor. Keeps about 2 months	Pickles, sauce, fresh eating	Early to late fall
Dolgo	Oval, solid bright red. Fruit a little small for pickles	Jelly, pickles. Best crab for sparkling red jelly	Late summer
Hyslop	Medium size, yellow, crimson shadings; fine firm flesh	Jelly, sauce, pickles	Early to mid-fall
Northland	Solid bright red, medium to large size, oval shape	Fresh eating, jelly, sauce pickles	Late summer
Red River	Large red fruit	Fresh eating, sauce	Early to late fall
Rescue	Large, greenish-yellow with red	Fresh eating, jelly	Mid to late summer
Trail	Large, red-striped fruit	Jelly, fresh eating, sauce	Late summer, early fall
Whitney	Large, red-striped, juicy. Tender flesh becomes mealy	Pickles, fresh eating, sauce	Late summer
Young America	Large, attractive red fruit	Fresh eating, jelly	Early fall

*Availability of crabapples is limited to where they grow—in northern United States (primarily northern Great Plains) and Canada.

CHAPTER III

Tender Loving Care from Grower to You

You never need to worry about getting a wormy apple when you bite into one you've bought at your local market, orchard or roadside stand.

It's not by chance that these apples are a feast for the eye as well as the palate. Apple growing is no longer hit or miss, as it was on the frontier when the fruit was likely to be lopsided, often wormy and frequently very sour. Apple growing has become a science, called pomology. Although apples have been cultivated for thousands of years, horticulturists say that greater improvements have been made in the last 50 years than in all previous history because of modern technology.

Yet one of those advances in technology has come under attack by many Americans: the spraying with chemicals to combat insects and diseases which are among the worst enemies of the apple grower.

If Apples Weren't Sprayed

What would happen if apples in commercial orchards were not sprayed? Wormy apples, of course! Another result could be greatly reduced crops with consequent higher prices for the consumer.

Apples would cost about $5 a pound if they were pro-
duced without the use of pesticides, according to some
estimates. In experiments in Ohio when four different
varieties of trees were sprayed—Jonathan, Stayman,
Red Delicious and Golden Delicious—they produced
from 85 to 100 percent marketable fruit. But when
trees were not sprayed for two years, only Jonathan
had fruit, and it was not marketable. The unsprayed
trees and fruits were severely damaged by apple scab
and various insects. In other tests, unsprayed apple
trees yielded only two bushels of fruit each compared
with a harvest of eleven bushels from each of the
sprayed trees. By making it possible to grow more
fruit, as well as better quality fruit, pesticides play an
important role in controlling food costs.

Spraying has become a precise science. Since insect
pests and diseases attack apples at different stages in
development of the fruit, the grower must know exactly when to spray and with what. Different types of
sprays are necessary for other purposes, too—such as
the stop-drop sprays to prevent apples from dropping
just before harvest and causing huge losses. The cor-
rect materials must be applied at precisely the right
time. This is too big a job to be done by hand, so the
grower must use powerful machines to cover the trees
thoroughly with the protective mist.

But how can you be sure that the pesticides won't
harm the food you eat? The answer is that federal
agencies keep a vigilant eye on their use. The chemicals are tested in the laboratory and in the field for
safe use. Tolerances have been set—standards for the
safe level of chemical residue that may remain on the
fruit when harvested. This is an almost infinitesimal
amount, usually stated as parts per million. You, yourself, can take further precautions by washing apples
before eating them.

Many other jobs are necessary to produce those beautiful apples for you. Once the orchard is planted the trees must be pruned in late winter each year to give the fruit better color and size, and to make spraying and harvesting easier. Then the trees must be fertilized so they will bear well, and they must be pollinated.

When the apple trees burst into bloom and the orchard is a pink and white fairyland, the grower brings in hives of honey bees to speed pollination. The reason: to insure a crop of well developed apples.

Essentially all commercial apple varieties are unable to produce fruit from their own pollen. To provide necessary cross-pollination, a grower may plant one Golden Delicious or Jonathan tree among ten Red Delicious trees. If the bees don't do their job of pollination satisfactorily, you might get a lopsided apple!

Intensive Work Before Harvest

Cultivation, irrigation (in some areas) and spraying when necessary follow blossomtime. Early in the growing period the orchardist must thin out half or two-thirds of the tiny green apples if the bloom has been heavy. Thinning is one of the most vital jobs if the grower is to harvest a crop of large, well formed, richly colored apples. Also, with thinning, food reserves will be conserved to produce fruit buds for next year's crop.

Although machines are used for many purposes in the orchard, harvesting the fruit must be done by hand by skilled pickers. Again, proper timing is crucial. Once apples are harvested, people and machines work together to do the washing, sorting and grading of the fruit, packing and storing before market.

Thus the top quality fruit you enjoy today is the result of a large capital investment along with intensive work in planting, cultivating, pruning, pollinating, controlling insects and diseases, thinning and harvesting, storing, packing and marketing. The grower needs patience, too—the patience to wait at least four or five years for young trees to come into bearing, and eight or nine years before the orchard can be considered profitable.

You can see that those perfectly shaped red and golden-yellow apples you buy are the products of thousands of hours of tender loving care by growers, so that you as a consumer can have the very best.

CHAPTER IV

Good to Eat, and Good for You, Too

Aroma and taste combine to make apples among the most appealing of fruits. Their spicy fragrance and delicious flavor whet your appetite.

But they have many other virtues. Their low calorie content makes them welcome in the diets of the weight conscious. Depending on variety, a medium size apple counts only 75 to 85 calories. Apples are a perfect snack food because their natural fruit sugars provide quick energy, while the bulky pulp gives you a filled-up feeling. Nor do individuals on low-sodium diets need to restrain themselves from eating apples; they contain very little sodium.

Apples are a source of Vitamins A and C, thiamin, riboflavin and niacin, small amounts of calcium, phosphorus, potassium and some copper, iron and manganese. However, the amount of Vitamin C (ascorbic acid) you get from an apple will vary depending on when and how you eat it.

According to nutritionists in the Agricultural Research Service of the U.S. Department of Agriculture, a large summer apple furnishes about 22 milligrams of Vitamin C if eaten whole, but only 14 milligrams if peeled. A fall or winter apple of the same large size has about 14 to 15 milligrams of Vitamin C if eaten whole, but only 5 to 7 milligrams if you peel it. After storage, the amount of Vitamin C drops as much as half.

Apples help keep you regular. The pectin in apples combines with water to form non-irritating bulk which helps intestinal activity—digestion and elimination.

Apples are thirst-quenchers too—they're 85 percent water. Little wonder that backpackers and football fans tuck apples into their pockets, and brown-baggers include them in their lunches. One apple is said to have the thirst slaking capability of half a glass of water.

While many fruits can be obtained only seasonally in our markets apples are available the year round. So it's quite possible for you to have that "apple a day" to "keep the doctor away." Of course, confirmed apple eaters will tell you they eat apples for the sheer enjoyment of this flavorful, satisfying fruit. Perhaps that's the best argument there is for apples.

CHAPTER V

Preserving Apples

It happens every other year in your backyard. Your
apple trees are loaded with beautiful fruit. Of course
you're delighted, but how can you use all those apples—
not let any go to waste? You give some to the neigh-
bors, the family eats them fresh every day, you bake
pies, cakes, cobblers, crisps—until the family exclaims,
"Not another apple dessert!"

There are many other possibilities for using apples—
the versatility of this fruit is amazing. You may want
to declare a moratorium on apple desserts, but not on
applesauce. Keep some in the refrigerator to spoon
over pancakes or French toast, or flavor it to serve
with meats (see Applesauce recipe).

To preserve apple goodness for winter use, make
that spicy Pennsylvania Dutch favorite, apple butter.
Or try our recipes for apple jellies, pickles and chutney.
Can some applesauce, too; and freeze apples for pie—or
freeze the pies, already baked.

Should you make apple juice or cider from your
surplus apples? It's possible, certainly, but it's a
complicated process and you'd probably be happier
buying it commercially produced.

Here are basic directions for canning and freezing
apples. Recipes for apple preserves are in Chapter VI.

Making Apple Jelly

The secret to success in jelly making is to prepare small amounts: about 4 c. juice at one time. NEVER double the recipe!

Wash jelly glasses in warm, soapy water and rinse with hot water. Keep them hot in hot water until you are ready to use them, so they won't break when filled with the hot jelly.

Pour hot jelly into hot glasses to within ½ inch of the top and cover immediately with paraffin which has been melted over hot water. Use about 1 tblsp. paraffin for 1 6-ounce glass—or just enough to make a layer about ⅛ inch thick. Prick any air bubbles to insure a good seal.

Let jelly stand overnight after sealing. In the morning, cover glasses with metal or paper lids. Label, date and store in a cool, dry place.

Canning Apples

Check the Apple Chart to see what varieties are best for pie and sauce; or use your backyard apples.

Canned apples will keep without sugar, though most fruits have better color, flavor and texture when canned with sugar or a sugar syrup.

To can applesauce, make the sauce your usual way or use our recipe. Sweeten it or not, as you wish, and pack hot in hot jars to ¼ inch of the top. Process pints and quarts for 20 minutes in a boiling water bath.

To can apples for pie, peel, core and cut apples into pieces or slices. To prevent darkening, drop cut apples into a solution of 1 gallon water to 2 tblsp. each salt and vinegar. Do not soak more than 15 minutes. Drain, then boil for 5 minutes in a thin sugar syrup (recipe follows). This will help apples hold their shape better. Pack apples in hot jars. Cover with hot thin sugar syrup to ½ inch of jar top. Process in boiling water bath, pints and quarts 20 minutes.

To make thin sugar syrup, combine 2 c. sugar and 4 c. water. Bring to a boil; boil 5 minutes. Skim if necessary. Makes 5 cups.

To use canned apples in pie, drain them and mix with spices, adding sugar if needed. How much sugar depends on sweetness or tartness of apples and your family's preference.

Freezing Apples and Applesauce

Freezing tends to soften apple texture, so use firm-fleshed cooking varieties suitable for pie, and freeze them shortly after harvesting. Apples that have been in storage for long periods may darken more quickly after freezing.

Here are three methods for freezing apples for pie. You can store them for a year or longer in your freezer.

1. Peel apples, core and cut into pie slices. To prevent darkening, soak for 5 minutes in a solution of 1 tsp. sodium bisulfite (U.S.P. grade) dissolved in 1 gallon cold water; use a glass, earthenware, stainless steel or enamel container. (Two ounces of sodium bisulfite will treat 7 bushels of apples. Do NOT use sodium bisulf*ide* or sodium sulf*ate*.)

After the 5-minute dip, drain slices. Pack in sugar using 1 pound of sugar to 5-7 pounds apple slices (or 1 c. sugar to 10-12 cups apple slices). Sprinkle sugar evenly over slices and let stand until sugar dissolves in fruit juices. Stir carefully to coat each slice with sugar solution. Fill container, seal, label, date and freeze.

If you cannot get sodium bisulfite at your drug

store, use an ascorbic acid powder sold in supermarkets to prevent browning of fruit. Follow package directions; then pack slices in sugar as directed above.

2. Peel and slice apples; soak them in a weak brine solution for 15 minutes (½ c. salt to 1 gallon water). Drain and pack slices in freezer containers. Cover with sugar syrup—2 c. sugar and ½ tsp. crystalline ascorbic acid dissolved in 1 quart cold water. The ascorbic acid helps keep apples from darkening. Seal container, label, date and freeze.

3. If apples are in perfect condition and if you have room in your freezer, you can freeze apples whole. Wash but do not peel; pack 6 to 8 apples in a plastic bag. Label, date and freeze. Do not thaw. Run cold water over each apple and peel while still frozen; use immediately for pie or other cooked desserts. These apples will darken quickly if you thaw them.

To use frozen apple slices in pie, partially thaw and drain them. Sweeten with ¼ to ½ cup sugar, depending on sweetness or tartness of apples. Mix the sugar with spices and a little flour or other thickener, even if you don't usually thicken your fresh apple pies. Freezing breaks down the structure of apples; they're more juicy than fresh apples and you have to compensate for this.

To freeze applesauce, sweeten it to taste after cooking; then cool and pack in containers to within ¾ inch of top. Label, date and freeze.

Freezing Apple Pies

One of the most satisfying ways to preserve your surplus apples is in pie crust. It's great to have baked apple pies in your freezer, ready to serve when company drops in unexpectedly. Laboratory tests at the University of Minnesota show that baked pies freeze more satisfactorily than unbaked pies. You can keep a baked pie up to six months in your freezer; but use an unbaked pie within three months.

Prepare pies as usual (see recipes on pages 97 to 108). Cool baked pies rapidly; then place in the freezer unwrapped. Keep pie level while it is freezing. When frozen, wrap, label, date and return to freezer for storage. (Both baked and unbaked pies freeze faster when unwrapped, and they're easier to wrap after they're frozen.)

To serve a baked frozen apple pie, let it stand at room temperature for 20-30 minutes; then place on the lower shelf of a preheated 350° F. oven and heat until warm, about 30 minutes. If your pie pan is shiny lightweight aluminum, place on cookie sheet in the oven.

To bake a frozen unbaked pie, place it on the lower shelf of a preheated 450° F. oven. Bake for 10-15 minutes; then reduce heat to 400° F. Total baking time will be 10-20 minutes longer than regular baking time as specified in recipe.

Drying Apples

Drying is one of the oldest methods of food preservation. Today, it's done under considerably more hygienic conditions than those described in Chapter I.

You can dry apple slices in the sun if you have a few days of hot, dry, breezy weather. Or you can dry them with controlled low heat (140° F.) in an oven or dehydrator. Either method takes time and requires careful attention, particularly at the beginning and end of the drying. For an evenly dried product, slices must be stirred or turned on the drying trays. Under controlled heat, it will take approximately 6 hours. Sun drying may take several days, and you should be prepared to finish drying indoors if weather conditions change. Once started, drying should be continuous until enough moisture is removed to keep the fruit from spoiling.

For satisfactory dried apples, use varieties of good dessert or cooking quality. They should be mature but not soft. You will probably want to pretreat them with an antioxidant to prevent darkening.

For more detailed directions on drying procedures and equipment, check with the Agricultural Extension Service in your state. The Food Editors of *Farm Journal* have also written a book on the subject, *How to Dry Fruits and Vegetables at Home*, Countryside Press, 1975.

CHAPTER VI

Recipes

"And for the winter fireside meet
Between the andiron's straddling feet
The mug of cider simmered slow
The apples sputtered in a row. . ."

—John Greenleaf Whittier, Snow-Bound

Beverages

HOT SPICED CIDER

1 qt. apple juice or cider
1 c. water
¼ c. brown sugar, firmly
   packed

⅛ tsp. salt
1 stick cinnamon
6 whole cloves

   Mix ingredients together and heat, but do not boil. Let stand overnight. Reheat before serving. Makes 5 cups.

ROSY GLOW APPLE CIDER

2 qts. apple juice or cider
¼ c. red cinnamon candies

Heat juice and candies together. Serve hot. Makes 8 cups.

APPLE ORANGE COOLER

Chilled apple juice
Orange sherbet
Chilled ginger ale

Fill punch cups half full with chilled apple juice. Put a spoonful of orange sherbet into the cup and follow with ginger ale, poured in slowly, to make about three-fourths cupful of Cooler.

HOLLY BERRY PUNCH

2 c. apple juice, chilled	2 c. water
2 c. cranberry juice, chilled	1 c. sugar
	1 qt. ginger ale, chilled

Blend apple and cranberry juices together. Boil together the water and sugar. Cool. Add the juices. Just before serving add the ginger ale. Makes about 25 servings.

RUTH'S HOT SPICY HOLIDAY PUNCH

2 qts. apple juice	2 tblsp. honey
4 c. cranberry juice cocktail	2 tblsp. whole cloves
2 tblsp. lemon juice	2 (3-in.) cinnamon sticks, broken into pieces

Combine all ingredients. Heat to boiling. Reduce heat and simmer 30 minutes. Taste the punch. If it is too sour, add a little honey. If too sweet, add more lemon. If not spicy enough to suit, simmer longer.

Strain and serve hot from a glass pitcher or punch bowl. Makes 3 quarts.

MULLED APPLE JUICE

2 (46 oz.) cans apple juice   2 sticks cinnamon
1 (6 oz.) can frozen lemon-   1 tsp. whole cloves
   ade concentrate   2 or 3 red apples

Combine apple juice and lemonade concentrate in large saucepan. Add cinnamon and cloves, tied in a bag. Heat until juices start to simmer. Remove spice bag. Pour into heat-proof punch bowl. Float two or three red apples which have been studded with additional whole cloves. Serve hot. Makes about 24 servings.

WASSAIL BOWL

1 (46 oz.) can apple juice   1 c. orange juice
1 (46 oz.) can unsweet-   3 sticks cinnamon
   ened pineapple juice   1 tsp. whole cloves

Combine all ingredients in large saucepan. Heat to boiling; reduce heat and simmer 15 to 20 minutes. Remove from heat and strain. Pour hot wassail in heat-proof punch bowl. Garnish with slices of unpeeled apple, studded with cloves, if desired. Makes 24 servings.

PERCOLATOR HOT CIDER

3 (46 oz.) cans apple juice
3 sticks cinnamon, broken
 in pieces
1 tsp. whole cloves

Pour apple juice in 30-cup electric coffee maker. Put cinnamon and cloves in coffee maker basket. Perk gently as for coffee. Keep hot and serve from the coffee maker. Makes 24 servings.

CIDER SHERBET REFRESHER

2 qts. apple juice or cider
1 qt. lemon sherbet
1 (10 oz.) bottle lemon-lime
 carbonated beverage
Sprigs of mint

Pour the chilled apple juice over the sherbet which has been spooned into punch bowl. Just before serving, pour the carbonated beverage in gently. Garnish with sprigs of mint. Makes 12 servings.

SPICED APPLE TEA

1 (46 oz.) can apple juice
1 tblsp. honey
½ tsp. whole cloves

1 cinnamon stick, broken
in pieces
2 tea bags

In saucepan combine apple juice, honey and the spices. Bring to a boil. Remove from heat and add the tea bags. Cover and brew for 3 to 5 minutes. Remove the tea bags. Strain out spices. Serve in mugs. Makes 6 to 8 servings.

RED APPLE WINE PUNCH

½ c. sugar
½ c. water
1 lemon, thinly sliced
1 orange, thinly sliced
8 whole cloves

1 stick cinnamon
½ c. orange juice
2 c. apple juice
2 c. Burgundy or claret
wine

Mix together sugar, water, lemon and orange slices, cloves and cinnamon. Bring to a boil over low heat and simmer 5 minutes. Add the orange and apple juices and reheat. Add the wine and reheat but do not boil. Strain and serve at once. If you serve from a punch bowl, float the lemon and orange slices in the punch. Makes about 6 cups.

Breads

APPLESAUCE PECAN ROLLS

1 (13¾ oz.) pkg. roll mix	⅓ c. brown sugar, firmly
2 tblsp. sugar	packed
6 tblsp. butter	½ c. chopped pecans
1¾ c. applesauce	Cinnamon

Prepare roll mix according to directions on package, adding 2 tblsp. sugar. Cover; let rise until doubled in bulk. Meanwhile add 2 tblsp. butter to applesauce; cook 10 minutes to evaporate some of the liquid, stirring occasionally. Melt remaining 4 tblsp. butter in 9″ baking pan; add brown sugar; heat until dissolved.

Roll out dough to 17×9″ rectangle. Spread with cooled applesauce and sprinkle with pecans and cinnamon. Roll up jelly roll fashion. Cut in 1″ slices. Arrange cut side up in pan on sugar mixture. Cover; let rise until doubled in bulk.

Bake in 400° oven for 20-25 minutes or until golden brown. Serve hot. Makes 16 rolls.

APPLE BLUEBERRY BREAD

3 c. sifted flour
1 c. sugar
1 tblsp. baking powder
1 tsp. salt
½ tsp. ground nutmeg
2 eggs, beaten

1½ c. applesauce
¼ c. melted butter
2 c. blueberries
¼ c. flour
1 c. chopped peeled
  apples

Sift together 3 c. flour, sugar, baking powder, salt and nutmeg. Mix eggs, applesauce and melted butter. Combine the two mixtures. Toss blueberries with ¼ c. flour and fold into batter with apples. Pour batter into two 8½×4½×2½″ loaf pans. Bake in 350° oven 55 minutes or until done. Cool for 10 minutes; then remove from pans. Cool. Makes 2 loaves.

AUTUMN APPLE COFFEE CAKE

1 egg
⅓ c. sugar
1 c. sifted flour
1 tblsp. baking powder
½ tsp. salt
½ c. milk
1 c. quick-cooking oats

½ c. melted shortening
4 sliced peeled apples
¼ c. sugar
½ tsp. ground cinnamon
¼ tsp. ground nutmeg
2 tblsp. butter

Beat egg and ⅓ c. sugar together until creamy. Sift together flour, baking powder and salt. Add alternately with milk to egg mixture. Stir in oats and melted shortening. Spread half the batter in a greased 9″ round baking pan. Arrange apple slices over batter. Spread remaining batter over apple slices.

Combine ¼ c. sugar, cinnamon and nutmeg. Cut in butter until mixture is crumbly. Sprinkle over batter. Bake in 375° oven 30 minutes or until done. Makes 8 servings.

APPLE CHEESE SANDWICH BREAD

½ c. shortening
⅔ c. sugar
2 eggs, well beaten
1 c. ground apple
   (include peel)
2 c. sifted flour

1 tsp. baking powder
1 tsp. baking soda
½ tsp. salt
½ c. grated mild Cheddar
   cheese
¼ c. chopped walnuts

Cream together shortening and sugar. Add eggs and apple.

Sift together flour, baking powder, soda and salt. Add to creamed mixture, blending well. Add cheese and nuts. Pour into well-greased and floured 9×5×3″ loaf pan.

Bake in 350° oven 60-65 minutes. Cool for 10 minutes; then remove from pan. Cool well. Makes 1 loaf.

APPLESAUCE PUFFS

2 c. biscuit mix
¼ c. sugar
½ tsp. ground cinnamon
¾ c. applesauce
3 tblsp. milk

1 egg, slightly beaten
2 tblsp. salad oil
2 tblsp. melted butter
¼ c. sugar
¼ tsp. ground cinnamon

Combine biscuit mix, ¼ c. sugar and ½ tsp. cinnamon. Add applesauce, milk, egg and oil. Mix until moistened. Fill greased 2″ muffin pans two-thirds full.

Bake in 400° oven 12 minutes or until done. Cool slightly; remove. Dip tops in melted butter, then in ¼ c. sugar mixed with ¼ tsp. cinnamon. Makes 24 muffins.

APPLE MUFFINS

½ c. sugar
¼ c. shortening
1 tsp. salt
1 egg
1 c. milk
1½ c. sifted flour
¼ tsp. ground cinnamon

3 tsp. baking powder
1½ c. chopped peeled
  apples
½ c. sifted flour
¼ c. brown sugar, firmly
  packed
¼ tsp. ground cinnamon

Combine sugar, shortening and salt; add egg and beat well. Stir in milk. Sift together flour, ¼ tsp. cinnamon and baking powder. Stir the flour into other mixture and blend just until flour is moistened. Batter will be lumpy. Add chopped apples which have been coated with ½ c. flour. Blend carefully. Fill well-greased muffin tins about two-thirds full. Sprinkle with combined brown sugar and ¼ tsp. cinnamon.

Bake in 400° oven 20-25 minutes or until golden brown. Serve warm. Makes 12 muffins.

APPLE STREUSEL MUFFINS

2 c. sifted flour
½ c. sugar
3 tsp. baking powder
1 tsp. salt
½ c. butter
2 c. chopped peeled
apples

½ tsp. grated lemon rind
1 egg, beaten
⅔ c. milk
¼ c. chopped walnuts
2 tblsp. sugar
½ tsp. grated lemon rind

Sift together flour, ½ c. sugar, baking powder and salt into a large bowl. Cut in butter with a pastry blender until mixture is crumbly. Reserve ½ c. mixture for the streusel topping. Stir apple and ½ tsp. lemon rind into mixture in bowl. Add milk to egg and add to apple mixture; stir lightly until moist. Spoon into 12 greased muffin cups.

Blend the ½ c. reserved mixture with walnuts, 2 tblsp. sugar and ½ tsp. lemon rind. Sprinkle over batter in each muffin cup.

Bake in 425° oven 20 minutes or until golden brown. Serve warm. Makes 12 muffins.

APPLE PECAN KUCHEN

¾ c. sugar
¼ c. shortening
1 egg, slightly beaten
½ c. milk
1½ c. sifted flour
2 tsp. baking powder
½ tsp. salt
½ tsp. ground cinnamon
⅛ tsp. ground nutmeg
⅛ tsp. ground cloves

½ c. brown sugar, firmly
   packed
2 tblsp. flour
1 tsp. cinnamon
2 tblsp. melted butter
2 c. sliced peeled apples
3 tblsp. butter
4 tblsp. honey
¾ c. chopped pecans

Cream together sugar and shortening. Add egg and mix well. Stir in milk. Sift together flour, baking powder, salt, cinnamon, nutmeg and cloves. Stir into creamed mixture until smooth. Spread half of the batter in a greased 9″ baking dish.

Mix together brown sugar, 2 tblsp. flour, 1 tsp. cinnamon and 2 tblsp. melted butter. Sprinkle over batter; then arrange sliced apples over crumbs. Cover with remaining batter.

Mix together 3 tblsp. butter, honey and pecans. Sprinkle over top layer.

Bake in 375° oven 30-35 minutes or until golden brown. Makes 9 servings.

APPLESAUCE HONEY ROLLS

2 (1 lb.) loaves frozen
   bread dough
1 c. brown sugar, firmly
   packed
½ c. honey

3 tblsp. butter
4 tblsp. melted butter
½ c. applesauce
2 tblsp. brown sugar
¼ c. raisins

Allow dough to thaw in plastic bag. Let rise until doubled in bulk.

Mix brown sugar, honey and butter. Sprinkle mixture over the bottom of a 13 × 9" baking pan.

Place dough on lightly floured pastry board or sheet and roll or pat into a 14 × 12" rectangle. Combine 4 tblsp. butter, applesauce, 2 tblsp. brown sugar and raisins; spread evenly over dough. Roll and seal. Cut into slices about ½ to 1" thick. Place slices on honey mixture in pan.

Bake in 350° oven 30 minutes or until golden brown. Cool slightly and turn over onto a plate or tray. Makes 12 rolls.

APPLE HONEY BUNS

2 c. sifted flour	2 tblsp. brown sugar,
2 tsp. baking powder	firmly packed
½ tsp. salt	¼ c. sunflower seeds
½ c. butter	¼ c. raisins
1 egg, beaten	⅓ c. brown sugar, firmly
Milk	packed
2 tblsp. melted butter	¼ c. honey
¼ c. thick applesauce	2 tblsp. butter

Sift flour, baking powder and salt together. Cut in ½ c. butter. Add enough milk to egg to make ⅔ c. Slowly add to flour mixture to form a soft dough. Knead dough ½ minute and roll to 14 × 10″ rectangle. Mix together 2 tblsp. butter, applesauce, 2 tblsp. brown sugar, sunflower seeds and raisins. Spread over dough. Roll dough from long side and cut into 8 slices. Combine ⅓ c. brown sugar, honey and 2 tblsp. butter and heat enough to dissolve sugar. Spoon 1 tablespoonful topping into 8 large, greased muffin pans. Place slices flat side down in muffin pans. Brush tops with remaining topping mixture.

Bake in 400° oven 15-20 minutes. Sprinkle with sunflower seeds. Makes 8 buns.

APPLE APRICOT LOAF

⅔ c. boiling water
½ c. finely diced dried
   apricots
2 c. sifted flour
2½ tsp. baking powder
½ tsp. baking soda
½ tsp. salt
½ tsp. ground allspice

Milk
½ c. shortening
¾ c. sugar
1 egg
1½ c. finely diced
   peeled apples
½ c. chopped walnuts

Pour boiling water over apricots; let stand. Sift together flour, baking powder, soda, salt and allspice. Drain apricots, saving liquid; pat apricots dry with paper towels. Add enough milk to apricot liquid to make ⅔ c.

Cream shortening; add sugar gradually while continuing to beat. Beat in egg. Add dry ingredients alternately with liquid. Combine apples, apricots and walnuts; fold in. Spoon into well-greased 9×5×3″ loaf pan.

Bake in 350° oven 50 minutes or until loaf tests done. Turn out of pan. Cool. Loaf is easier to slice if it stands overnight. Makes 1 loaf.

QUICK APPLE COFFEE CAKE

2 tblsp. sugar
2 c. biscuit mix
1 egg
¾ c. milk
1½ c. finely chopped
   peeled apples
⅓ c. brown sugar, firmly
   packed

½ tsp. ground cinnamon
⅓ c. biscuit mix
¼ c. cold butter
½ c. chopped peeled
   apples

Combine sugar, 2 c. biscuit mix, egg, milk and apples; beat vigorously for 30 seconds. Spread batter in greased 9″ round baking pan.

Combine brown sugar, cinnamon and ⅓ c. biscuit mix. Cut in butter until crumbly. Add apples. Sprinkle over batter. Bake in 400° oven 25 minutes or until golden brown. Makes 8 to 10 servings.

APPLE DOUGHNUT BALLS

5 eggs	2 tsp. baking soda
2 c. sugar	1 tsp. salt
1 c. heavy cream	½ tsp. ground nutmeg
1¾ c. buttermilk	½ tsp. ground cinnamon
1½ grated peeled apples	1 tsp. vanilla
7 c. sifted flour	Cooking oil

Beat eggs. Add sugar; beat well. Stir in cream and buttermilk. Add apples. Sift together flour, baking soda, salt, nutmeg and cinnamon. Stir in egg mixture. Add vanilla.

Heat oil to 375°. Drop batter by teaspoonfuls into oil. Fry until brown. Drain on paper towels. Serve plain or sugared. Makes 11 dozen.

APPLE CINNAMON WAFFLES

1½ c. sifted flour	2 eggs, separated
½ tsp. salt	1 c. milk
¾ tsp. ground cinnamon	¾ c. grated peeled apples
1 tblsp. sugar	¼ c. melted butter
2 tsp. baking powder	

Sift together flour, salt, cinnamon, sugar and baking powder. Beat egg yolks; add milk. Combine with dry mixture. Add apples and melted butter. Beat egg whites until stiff; fold into batter. Bake until golden brown in hot waffle iron. Yields about 6 waffles.

APPLE DOUGHNUTS

1 pkg. active dry yeast
½ tsp. sugar
¾ c. warm milk
2 c. sifted flour
2 tblsp. sugar
⅛ tsp. salt
2 eggs, beaten
½ c. raisins

½ c. diced, peeled
  apples
3 tblsp. mixed candied
  fruit
1 tsp. grated lemon peel
Cooking oil
Confectioners sugar

Sprinkle yeast and ½ tsp. sugar on milk; stir to dissolve. Let stand 10 minutes.

Sift together flour, 2 tblsp. sugar and salt into bowl. Make a well in the center. Add yeast and eggs; mix just until blended. Stir in raisins, apples, candied fruit and lemon peel. Cover and let rise in warm place until doubled, about 1 hour.

Drop batter by heaping tablespoonfuls into deep hot oil (350°), frying until golden brown, about 3 minutes. Drain on paper towels. Dust with confectioners sugar. Makes 15.

APPLE PANCAKES

1½ c. sifted flour	1 egg, beaten
1½ tsp. baking powder	1¼ c. milk
¾ tsp. salt	2 tblsp. oil
1 tblsp. sugar	¾ c. grated peeled apples

Sift together flour, baking powder, salt and sugar. Combine egg, milk and oil. Add gradually to dry ingredients, stirring only until batter is smooth. Fold in apples.

Drop by spoonfuls onto hot greased griddle. Cook slowly until the surface is covered with bubbles. Turn and cook until the bottom is a delicate brown. Makes about 18 medium-size pancakes.

Bars and Cookies

DANISH PASTRY APPLE SQUARES

2¾ c. sifted flour
1 tsp. salt
1 c. shortening plus
   2 tblsp.
Milk
1 egg yolk, beaten
1 c. crushed corn flakes
8 c. sliced, peeled apples

⅔ c. sugar
½ tsp. ground cinnamon
1 egg white, stiffly beaten
1 c. sifted confectioners
   sugar
½ tsp. vanilla
1-2 tblsp. water

Sift together flour and salt. Cut in shortening until crumbly. Add enough milk to egg yolk to make ⅔ c. Add to flour mixture; mix to blend. Divide dough into two parts. Roll half of dough to fit a 15½ × 10½ × 1″ jelly roll pan. Sprinkle bottom crust with corn flakes. Combine apples, sugar and cinnamon, stirring gently. Spread apple mixture over bottom crust on top of corn flakes. Roll out other half of dough and place on top. Pinch edges together to seal. Beat egg white stiff and brush over top crust.

Bake in 400° oven 50-60 minutes or until golden. While pie squares are baking, mix together confectioners sugar, vanilla and water. Remove pie squares from oven at end of baking period and cool slightly. Frost when crust is still warm. Makes 16 servings.

APPLE OATMEAL BARS

2 c. sifted flour
1 tsp. salt
1 tsp. baking soda
1 c. brown sugar, firmly
   packed

1 c. quick-cooking oats
1 c. shortening
6 tblsp. butter
4 c. sliced, peeled apples
½ c. sugar

Sift together flour, salt and baking soda. Add brown sugar and oats; mix well. Cut in shortening until crumbly. Press half of crumbs in greased 13×9×2" baking pan. Dot with 4 tblsp. butter. Add apples and sprinkle with the ½ c. sugar. Cover with remaining crumb mixture and dot with the remaining 2 tblsp. butter.

Bake in 350° oven 40-45 minutes or until done. Makes 2½ dozen.

APPLE BARS

1 c. sifted flour
½ tsp. salt
½ tsp. baking soda
½ c. brown sugar, firmly
   packed
1 c. quick-cooking oats

½ c. shortening
2½ c. sliced, peeled
   apples
¼ c. sugar
2 tblsp. butter

Sift together flour, salt and baking soda. Add brown sugar and oats; mix well. Cut in shortening until mixture is crumbly. Press half of mixture in greased 8" square baking dish. Place apples over crumbs; sprinkle with sugar. Dot with butter. Sprinkle with the remaining crumb mixture.

Bake in 350° oven 40-45 minutes. Cut into bars. Serve cold as cookies or hot with pudding sauce as a dessert. Makes 12 servings.

SPICY APPLE SQUARES

1 c. brown sugar, firmly
   packed
¼ c. butter
1 egg
½ tsp. vanilla
¾ c. sifted flour
1 tsp. baking powder

¼ tsp. salt
¼ tsp. ground cinnamon
½ c. chopped nuts
1 c. finely diced,
   peeled apples
Confectioners sugar

Cream together brown sugar and butter until fluffy. Add egg and vanilla; beat well. Sift together flour, baking powder, salt and cinnamon. Add to creamed mixture; mix well. Add nuts and apples. Spread in well-greased and floured 8" square baking pan.

Bake in 350° oven 25 minutes or until done. Do not overbake. Cut into squares. Before serving, dust with sifted confectioners sugar. Makes 16 servings.

APPLE WALNUT BROWNIES

½ c. butter
2 (1 oz.) sq. unsweet-
   ened chocolate
2 eggs
1 c. sugar
1 c. sifted flour

½ tsp. baking powder
¼ tsp. salt
1 c. chopped nuts
1½ c. finely chopped,
   peeled apples
1 tsp. vanilla

Melt butter and chocolate together over hot water. Beat eggs until light and lemon-colored; add sugar gradually while continuing to beat. Stir in the chocolate mixture. Beat for 1 minute. Sift together flour, baking powder and salt; stir into chocolate mixutre. Add nuts, apples and vanilla. Spoon into greased 8″ square baking pan.

Bake in 350° oven 35-40 minutes or until done. Makes 16 servings.

APPLE DREAM BARS

1 c. sifted flour	2 c. peeled, diced apples
¼ c. sugar	¼ c. chopped almonds
6 tblsp. butter	½ c. sifted flour
2 eggs	1 tsp. baking powder
1 c. brown sugar, firmly	¼ tsp. salt
packed	¼ tsp. ground nutmeg

Combine flour and sugar. Cut in butter until crumbly. Press in 8" square baking pan.

Bake in 350° oven 20 minutes or until lightly browned.

Beat eggs until thick and lemon-colored. Stir in brown sugar, vanilla, apples and almonds. Sift together flour, baking powder, salt and nutmeg. Stir into egg mixture. Spread over bottom layer.

Bake in 350° oven 30 minutes or until apples are tender and the crust is a golden brown. Makes 16 servings.

APPLE MOLASSES BARS

1 c. butter
½ c. brown sugar, firmly packed
1 c. sugar
½ c. molasses
2 eggs
1 c. applesauce
3 c. sifted flour
2 tsp. baking powder
½ tsp. baking soda
½ tsp. salt
½ tsp. ground cinnamon
½ c. dairy sour cream
1 (3 oz.) pkg. cream cheese, softened
¼ c. butter, softened
1⅔ c. sifted confectioners sugar
1 tblsp. cream or milk
1 tsp. vanilla

Cream together butter, sugars and molasses. Add eggs, one at a time, beat well. Add applesauce. Sift together flour, baking powder, baking soda, salt and cinnamon. Add alternately with sour cream; mix well. Spread in greased 15½ × 10½ × 1″ jelly roll pan.

Bake in 350° oven 25-30 minutes or until done. When cool, frost with a cream cheese frosting. Blend together cheese and butter. Add confectioners sugar, cream and vanilla. Beat mixture until smooth. Makes about 3 dozen bars.

APPLE CHIP COOKIES

1 c. shortening	1 tsp. ground cinnamon
1½ c. brown sugar,	¼ tsp. ground cloves
firmly packed	¼ tsp. ground nutmeg
¼ c. light molasses	¾ c. chopped walnuts
3 eggs	1 c. finely chopped,
3½ c. sifted flour	peeled apples
½ tsp. salt	1 (6 oz.) pkg. semi-sweet
1 tsp. baking soda	chocolate chips

Cream together shortening and brown sugar until light and fluffy; add molasses. Add eggs, one at a time, beating well after each addition. Sift together flour, salt, baking soda, cinnamon, cloves and nutmeg. Add to creamed mixture, mixing well. Stir in nuts, apples and chocolate chips. Mix well. Drop by teaspoonfuls on greased baking sheet.

Bake in 350° oven 12-15 minutes, or until done. Makes 6 dozen.

APPLE CHIP OATMEAL COOKIES

1 c. shortening
1 c. brown sugar, firmly
  packed
1 c. sugar
2 eggs
2 tblsp. water
1 tsp. vanilla
1½ c. sifted flour

1 tsp. baking soda
1 tsp. salt
3 c. quick-cooking oats
1 c. chocolate or butter-
  scotch chips
1 c. chopped, peeled
  apples
½ c. chopped nuts

Cream together shortening and sugars. Add eggs, one at a time, beating well. Add water and vanilla. Sift together flour, baking soda and salt. Add to creamed mixture; mixing well. Add oats, chips, apples and nuts. Drop by teaspoonfuls onto greased baking sheet.

Bake in 375° oven 10-12 minutes or until done. Makes about 8 dozen.

APPLE CEREAL COOKIES

1 c. butter
1 c. sugar
1 c. brown sugar, firmly
   packed
2 eggs
1½ c. whole wheat flour
1½ c. sifted flour
1 tsp. salt

1 tsp. baking soda
1 tsp. ground cinnamon
¼ tsp. ground cloves
¼ tsp. ground allspice
1 c. grated, peeled apple
1 c. granola
1 c. quick-cooking oats
1 c. raisins

Cream together butter and sugars until fluffy. Add eggs, one at a time, beating well. Combine flours, salt, baking soda, cinnamon, cloves and allspice. Add to creamed mixture; mix well. Add grated apple, cereal, oats and raisins. Drop by teaspoonfuls onto greased baking sheets.

Bake in 350° oven about 15 minutes or until done. Makes about 6 dozen.

APPLESAUCE DATE NUT COOKIES

¾ c. butter
½ c. sugar
½ c. brown sugar, firmly
    packed
1 egg
1 c. applesauce
2 c. sifted flour
1 tsp. baking powder

½ tsp. baking soda
¼ tsp. salt
½ tsp. ground cinnamon
¼ tsp. ground nutmeg
¾ c. cut up dates
½ c. chopped nuts
1 tsp. vanilla

Cream together shortening and sugars until fluffy. Add egg and mix thoroughly. Sift together flour, baking powder, baking soda, salt, cinnamon and nutmeg. Add to creamed mixture alternately with applesauce, blending well. Add dates, nuts and vanilla. Drop by teaspoonfuls on greased baking sheets about 1½ inches apart.

Bake in 400° oven about 10 minutes or until brown. Makes about 3 dozen cookies.

Cakes

DIXIE'S FRESH APPLE CAKE

2 c. brown sugar, firmly packed	1 tsp. ground cinnamon
1 c. butter	1 c. cold coffee
2 eggs	1 c. chopped walnuts
3 c. sifted flour	1 c. raisins
2 tsp. baking soda	2 c. diced peeled apples
1 tsp. baking powder	½ c. sugar
½ tsp. salt	¼ c. brown sugar, firmly packed
½ tsp. ground nutmeg	½ tsp. ground cinnamon
¼ tsp. ground cloves	½ c. chopped nuts

Cream together 2 c. brown sugar and butter until fluffy. Add eggs, one at a time, beating after each addition. Sift together flour, baking soda, baking powder, salt, nutmeg, cloves and 1 tsp. cinnamon. Add dry ingredients alternately with the coffee, blending well. Add apples, raisins and walnuts. Spread in greased 13×9×2″ baking pan.

Combine sugar, ¼ c. brown sugar, ½ tsp. cinnamon and nuts; blend well. Sprinkle topping on batter and gently press into batter.

Bake in 350° oven 45 minutes or until done. Makes 20 servings.

SOUR CREAM APPLE CAKE

3 c. sifted flour	2 eggs
1 c. sugar	2 c. diced, peeled apples
4 tsp. baking powder	1 c. dairy sour cream
1 tsp. salt	2 eggs, slightly beaten
1 tsp. ground cinnamon	½ c. sugar
1 c. milk	1 c. chopped walnuts
½ c. soft butter	

Sift together flour, sugar, baking powder, salt and cinnamon. Add milk, butter and 2 eggs. Beat until smooth. Stir in apples and pour into greased 13×9×2″ baking pan.

Blend together sour cream and 2 eggs. Spread over batter. Sprinkle with combined ½ c. sugar and nuts.

Bake in 375° oven for 30-35 minutes or until done. Makes 16 servings.

FINNISH APPLE SUGAR CAKE

¼ c. butter	¼ tsp. salt
1 c. sugar	¾ c. light cream
2 eggs	2 c. sliced, peeled apples
2 c. sifted flour	3 tblsp. sugar
1 ½ tsp. baking powder	1 tsp. ground cinnamon

Cream together butter and 1 c. sugar thoroughly. Add eggs, beat until light and fluffy. Sift flour with baking powder and salt; add alternately with cream. Mix until batter is smooth. Spread in well-greased 9″ square baking pan. Place apple slices in rows over cake with outer edges up. Combine 3 tblsp. sugar and cinnamon; sprinkle evenly over the cake.

Bake in 350° oven 40-45 minutes or until done. Makes 9 servings.

MINNESOTA APPLE UPSIDE DOWN CAKE

4 c. sliced, peeled apples	1 tsp. salt
1 c. sugar	½ c. shortening
2 tblsp. butter	1 c. sugar
½ tsp. ground cinnamon	2 eggs
2 c. sifted flour	1 c. milk
2½ tsp. baking powder	1 tsp. vanilla

Combine apples, 1 c. sugar, butter and cinnamon in saucepan. Cook until tender, stirring frequently. Pour into well-greased 13×9×2″ baking pan.

Sift together flour, baking powder and salt. Cream together shortening with sugar. Blend in eggs, one at a time, beating well. Combine milk and vanilla; add alternately with dry ingredients to creamed mixture, beginning and ending with dry ingredients. Spread over apples in pan.

Bake in 350° oven 35-40 minutes or until done. Remove from oven. Turn cake upside down over large serving plate. Let stand a few minutes; then remove pan. Makes 16 servings.

SPICY APPLE COFFEE CAKE

½ c. butter
1⅓ c. sugar
2 eggs, beaten
1 tsp. salt
¼ tsp. ground allspice
¼ tsp. ground nutmeg
¼ tsp. ground cinnamon
2½ c. chopped, peeled
   apples
⅓ c. raisins

2 c. sifted flour
1 tsp. baking powder
¼ tsp. baking soda
⅓ c. water
3 tblsp. butter
¾ c. brown sugar, firmly
   packed
3 tblsp. milk
1¼ tsp. light corn syrup
⅓ c. chopped nuts

Combine ½ c. butter, sugar, eggs, salt, allspice, nutmeg and cinnamon. Mix well. Stir in apples and raisins. Sift together flour, baking powder and baking soda. Add to first mixture. Stir in water. Spread in wellgreased 9″ square baking pan.

Bake in 350° oven 40 minutes or until done.

Combine 3 tblsp. butter, brown sugar, milk and corn syrup in saucepan and bring to a boil. Remove from heat and add nuts. Pour over hot baked cake. Makes 9-12 servings.

ROSY APPLE CAKE

1 c. shortening
1 c. sugar
4 eggs
1 tsp. vanilla
2 c. sifted flour
½ tsp. salt

1 tsp. grated lemon peel
4 c. sliced, unpeeled
   apples
½ c. sugar
½ tsp. ground cinnamon
4 tblsp. butter

Cream together shortening and 1 cup of sugar until light and fluffy. Beat in eggs, one at a time, beating well after each addition. Add vanilla. Sift together flour and salt; add grated lemon peel. Beat well. Spread into greased 13 × 9 × 2″ baking pan.

Place apples in rows on batter. Combine ½ c. sugar and cinnamon; sprinkle over apples. Dot with butter.

Bake in 350° oven for 40–45 minutes or until done. Makes 16 servings.

APPLE WHOLE WHEAT CAKE

1 c. shortening	4 tsp. baking powder
1 c. brown sugar, firmly packed	½ tsp. salt
1 c. sugar	1 c. milk
4 eggs	¼ c. cold coffee
1½ c. whole wheat flour	4 c. sliced, peeled apples
1½ c. sifted flour	⅓ c. sugar
	½ tsp. ground cinnamon

Cream together shortening, brown sugar and 1 c. sugar until light. Add eggs, one at a time, beating well after each addition. Sift together flours, baking powder and salt. Add flour mixture alternately with the milk and coffee. (Do NOT overbeat!) Place half of mixture in greased and lightly floured 13×9×2″ baking pan. Place half the apple slices in about 3 rows on top. Add the remaining batter and then the rest of the apple slices. Sprinkle with combined ⅓ c. sugar and cinnamon.

Bake in 350° oven 45-50 minutes or until done. Makes 16 servings.

APPLE BLUEBERRY CAKE

¾ c. butter
1½ c. sugar
4 eggs
3 c. sifted flour
1½ tsp. baking powder
¾ tsp. salt
1½ tsp. baking soda
1½ c. dairy sour cream

1½ tsp. vanilla
1 tsp. ground cardamom
2 c. chopped, peeled
   apples
1 c. blueberries
½ c. brown sugar, firmly
   packed

Cream together butter and sugar until fluffy. Add eggs, one at a time, beating well after each addition. Sift together flour, baking powder, salt and baking soda. Add to creamed mixture, alternating with the sour cream. Stir in vanilla and cardamom. Fold in the chopped apple. Pour half the batter into a well-greased and lightly floured 13 × 9 × 2″ baking pan. Cover with blueberries. Sprinkle with brown sugar. Top with remaining batter.

Bake in 325° oven 40-50 minutes or until done. Cool on cake rack. Makes 16 servings.

APPLE GRAHAM CRACKER CAKE

5 tblsp. butter	¾ c. milk
½ c. sugar	1½ tsp. vanilla
3 egg yolks	3 egg whites
3 c. graham cracker	6 c. sliced, peeled apples
crumbs	3 tblsp. butter, melted
2 tsp. baking powder	2 tblsp. sugar
¼ tsp. salt	¾ tsp. ground cinnamon

Cream together butter and ½ c. sugar until light. Add egg yolks; beat well. Combine graham cracker crumbs, baking powder and salt; add alternately with milk and vanilla to other ingredients, stirring until well-blended. Beat egg whites until stiff; fold into cake mixture. Pour half of cake batter into greased 8″ square baking dish. Cover with a layer of apples. Pour remainder of mixture over apples. Arrange remaining apples on top of batter and cover with melted butter. Sprinkle with combined 2 tblsp. sugar and cinnamon.

Bake in 350° oven for 45 minutes or until done. Makes 8 servings.

APPLE LEMON SAUCE CAKE

2 c. sugar	½ tsp. salt
½ c. butter	⅛ tsp. ground cloves
2 eggs	4 c. grated, peeled apples
2½ c. sifted flour	1 c. chopped nuts
2 tsp. baking soda	1 c. raisins
1 tsp. ground cinnamon	Lemon Sauce
½ tsp. ground nutmeg	(recipe follows)

Cream together butter and sugar until light. Add eggs; beat well. Sift together flour, baking soda, cinnamon, nutmeg, salt and cloves. Add alternately with grated apple, mixing well after each addition. Blend in nuts and raisins. Spread in greased 13×9×2″ baking pan.

Bake in 350° oven 45 minutes or until done. Serve warm with Lemon Sauce over cake. Makes 16 servings.

Lemon Sauce: Mix 4 tsp. cornstarch, ½ c. sugar, ⅛ tsp. salt and ¼ tsp. nutmeg in small saucepan. Gradually stir in 1 c. water. Cook, stirring constantly, until mixture thickens and boils. Boil and stir 1 minute. Remove from heat. Stir in 1 tsp. grated lemon peel, 2 tblsp. lemon juice and 2 tblsp. butter.

EASY APPLE SPICE CAKE

1 (18½ oz.) pkg. spice cake mix	¼ c. butter, melted
⅔ c. water	1 tsp. vanilla
1 egg	2 c. sliced, peeled apples
¼ tsp. ground cinnamon	2 tblsp. butter

Blend half a package (approximately 2¼ c.) cake mix, water and egg in mixing bowl. Beat at medium speed until batter is smooth. Pour half the batter into a greased 9″ square pan. Combine remaining cake mix with cinnamon; add melted butter and vanilla. Toss with a fork to form large crumbs. Sprinkle half of crumb mixture over batter in pan. Arrange 1 c. of apple slices over crumb mixture. Carefully spoon on remaning batter. Arrange rest of apple slices over batter. Dot with the butter and sprinkle with remaining crumb mixture.

Bake in 350° oven 40-45 minutes or until done. Serve warm. Makes 9 servings.

GINGER APPLE UPSIDE DOWN CAKE

¼ c. butter
¾ c. brown sugar, firmly
   packed

3 medium apples
1 (14 oz.) pkg. ginger-
   bread cake mix

Melt butter in 8″ square baking pan. Add brown sugar and stir until dissolved. Peel and core apples. Cut each apple in half to make two thick rings. Arrange rings on butter and sugar mixture.

Prepare cake mix according to package directions. Pour batter over apples.

Bake in 350° oven 40-45 minutes or until done. Cool 5 minutes; then turn upside down on serving plate. Serve warm with whipped cream. Makes 6 to 8 servings.

APPLESAUCE CAKE WITH APPLE
JUICE FROSTING

1 (18½ oz.) pkg. yellow
   cake mix
½ tsp. ground nutmeg
½ tsp. ground allspice
1 tsp. ground cinnamon

1½ c. applesauce
2 eggs
¾ c. chopped walnuts
Fluffy Apple Juice Frost-
   ing (recipe follows)

Combine cake mix, nutmeg, allspice and cinnamon. Add applesauce and eggs. Beat 3 minutes, until smooth and creamy. Stir in chopped walnuts. Pour into 2 greased and floured 8″ layer cake pans.

Bake in 350° oven 25-30 minutes or until cake tests done. Cool and frost with Fluffy Apple Juice Frosting. Make 16 servings.

Fluffy Apple Juice Frosting: Mix 1½ c. sugar, ¾ c. apple juice and ⅛ tsp. salt in 2-qt. saucepan. Cook until the syrup forms a soft ball (234° to 240° F.) when a little of it is dropped into a cup of cold water. Pour very slowly over 3 stiffly beaten egg whites, beating constantly. Continue beating until mixture stands in soft peaks. Spread between layers and over the top and sides of cake.

SIMPLE SIMON CAKE

1½ c. sifted flour
¼ c. cocoa
1 c. sugar
1 tsp. baking soda
½ tsp. salt

1 tsp. cider vinegar
1 tsp. vanilla
5 tblsp. oil
1½ c. applesauce

Sift together flour, cocoa, sugar, baking soda and salt into greased 8″ square baking pan. Make three depressions in dry ingredients. Pour vinegar into one, vanilla into a second and oil into the third. Spoon applesauce over all. Mix well until smooth.

Bake in 350° oven for 35 minutes. When cool cut into squares. Top with whipped cream or applesauce. Makes 8 servings.

APPLESAUCE DATE CAKE

2 c. sifted flour
2 tsp. baking soda
1 tsp. ground cinnamon
½ tsp. ground allspice
½ tsp. ground nutmeg
¼ tsp. ground cloves
¼ tsp. salt
2 eggs

1 c. brown sugar, firmly
    packed
½ c. butter
2 c. hot applesauce
1 c. chopped dates
½ c. chopped walnuts
Cream Cheese Frosting
    (recipe follows)

Sift flour with soda, spices and salt. Add eggs, sugar, butter and 1 cup of the hot applesauce. Beat until ingredients are combined. Then beat 2 minutes longer, occasionally scraping sides of bowl. Add remaining applesauce, the dates and walnuts. Beat 1 minute. Pour batter into greased and lightly floured 9″ square pan.

Bake in 350° oven 40-50 minutes. Cool in pan 10 minutes. Remove from pan and cool on wire rack. Frost with Cream Cheese Frosting. Makes 9-12 servings.

Cream Cheese Frosting: Combine 1 (3 oz.) pkg. cream cheese, 1 tblsp. butter, 1 tsp. vanilla and 2 c. sifted confectioner's sugar. Beat until smooth and fluffy. Spread on cake.

APPLESAUCE CHOCOLATE CUP CAKES

½ c. butter	½ tsp. salt
1 c. sugar	½ tsp. baking powder
1 egg	¼ tsp. ground allspice
1¾ c. sifted flour	1½ squares unsweetened
1 tsp. baking soda	chocolate, grated
1 tsp. ground cinnamon	1¼ c. applesauce

Cream together butter and sugar until light. Add egg; beat well. Sift together flour, baking soda, cinnamon, salt, baking powder and allspice. Add chocolate. Add flour mixture alternately with applesauce, beating well each time. Fill paper-lined cupcake pans two-thirds full.

Bake in 375° oven 20 minutes or until done. Makes 18 cupcakes.

Desserts

BAKED APPLES

Whole apples   Ground cinnamon or
Sugar   nutmeg
Butter   1 c. water

Select good-quality baking apples of uniform size. Wash and core, but do not cut through to the blossom end. Peel the upper fourth or third of each apple.

Place apples in oblong baking dish. In the center of each apple put 1 to 2 tblsp. sugar and ½ tsp. butter. Sprinkle apples with cinnamon or nutmeg.

Pour 1 c. water around the apples (or to the depth of ½"). Cover with aluminum foil.

Bake in 350° oven 45-60 minutes or until done. Serve warm or cold.

APPLE COCONUT CRUSTED DESSERT

7½ c. sliced, peeled   ¼ c. orange juice
   apples   ½ c. brown sugar,
½ c. brown sugar,   firmly packed
   firmly packed   6 tblsp. butter
1½ tsp. ground cinnamon   ⅓ c. flour
¼ tsp. ground mace   ½ c. coconut
3 tblsp. flour

Arrange apples in greased 8" square baking pan. Combine ½ c. brown sugar, cinnamon, mace and 3 tblsp. flour; mix well. Sprinkle over apples. Pour orange juice evenly over all.

Combine ½ c. brown sugar and ⅓ c. flour. Cut in butter until crumbly. Stir in coconut. Sprinkle over apples. Cover with aluminum foil.

Bake in 425° oven 20 minutes. Remove foil; bake 15 more minutes. Makes 6 to 8 servings.

CREAMY APPLE CHEESE DESSERT

---

1 c. sifted flour	**¼ tsp. ground cinnamon**
1 tblsp. sugar	**¼ tsp. ground nutmeg**
⅛ tsp. salt	**1 (3 oz.) pkg. cream**
¼ c. butter	**cheese, softened**
1 egg yolk, beaten	**½ c. sugar**
1 tsp. water	**2 eggs, beaten**
2½ c. canned apple	**⅛ tsp. salt**
slices, drained	**½ c. heavy cream**
⅓ c. sugar	**1 tsp. vanilla**

Combine flour, 1 tblsp. sugar and ⅛ tsp. salt. Cut in butter until crumbly. Combine 1 egg yolk and water; stir into crumb mixture. Press in bottom and sides of 8″ square baking pan.

Combine apples, ⅓ c. sugar, cinnamon and nutmeg; mix well. Arrange apples in crust.

Bake in 425° oven 10 minutes.

Whip cream cheese until smooth. Beat in ½ c. sugar, 2 eggs and ⅛ tsp. salt. Blend in cream and vanilla; mix well. Pour evenly over apples.

Reduce oven to 350° Bake 30-35 more minutes or until set. Cool and then chill. Serve with whipped cream, if you wish. Makes 8 servings.

AMBER APPLES

2 lbs. firm apples
  (about 6 medium)

1 (46 oz.) can apple juice
Vanilla ice cream

Peel and core apples. Cut into eighths.

Pour apple juice in a large skillet. Add apples in a single layer. Cook very slowly, basting occasionally, until apples are translucent and a deep amber color. Add a little water or more juice if syrup becomes too thick.

Lift slices carefully from juice and arrange in a pretty glass serving dish. Chill and serve with vanilla ice cream. Makes 6 servings.

APPLE CHEESE CRISP

6½ c. sliced, peeled
  apples
1 c. sugar
½ c. sifted flour
¼ tsp. salt

⅛ tsp. ground cinnamon
¼ c. butter
⅔ c. shredded Cheddar
  cheese

Arrange apples in 9″ pie plate. Sprinkle with ½ c. sugar. Combine remaining ½ c. sugar, flour, salt and cinnamon. Cut in butter until crumbly. Add cheese; mix well. Sprinkle over apples.

Bake in 350° oven 40-45 minutes or until apples are tender. Serve warm or cold. Makes 6 to 8 servings.

OATMEAL APPLE CRUNCH

6 c. sliced, peeled apples   ¼ tsp. ground cinnamon
1 c. sifted flour   1 c. butter
1 c. brown sugar,   1 c. quick-cooking oats
   firmly packed   ¼ c. chopped walnuts

Arrange apples in greased 8″ square baking dish. Combine flour, brown sugar and cinnamon. Cut in butter until crumbly. Add oats and walnuts; mix well. Sprinkle over apples.

Bake in 350° oven 50-60 minutes or until apples are tender. Serve warm. Makes 9 servings.

APPLE CRANBERRY CRISP

4½ c. sliced, peeled   1 c. brown sugar,
   apples   firmly packed
¾ c. whole cranberry   1 tsp. ground cinnamon
   sauce   6 tblsp. butter
¾ c. sifted flour

Arrange apples in greased 8″ baking dish. Spread cranberry sauce on top. Combine flour, brown sugar and cinnamon. Cut in butter until crumbly. Sprinkle over apple mixture.

Bake in 350° oven 35-40 minutes or until apples are tender. Serve warm or cold. Makes 6-8 servings.

GRANDMOTHER'S APPLE TAPIOCA PUDDING

½ c. sugar
¼ tsp. salt
2 c. water

2 c. sliced, peeled apples
2 tblsp. quick-cooking
tapioca

Add sugar and salt to water in 2-qt. saucepan. Place over medium heat and stir until sugar is dissolved. Add apples and cover. Cook slowly until apples are tender, about 15 minutes. Carefully stir in tapioca, continuing to cook until tapioca is transparent.

Serve cold with whipped cream, if you wish. Makes 4 servings.

APPLE PIZZA PIE

1¼ c. sifted flour
1 tsp. salt
½ c. shortening
1 c. shredded Cheddar
cheese
¼ c. iced water
½ c. powdered non-
dairy creamer
½ c. brown sugar,
firmly packed

½ c. sugar
⅓ c. sifted flour
¼ tsp. salt
1 tsp. ground cinnamon
½ tsp. ground nutmeg
¼ c. butter
6 c. sliced, peeled apples
(½" thick)
2 tblsp. lemon juice

Combine 1¼ c. flour and 1 tsp. salt. Cut in shortening until crumbly. Add cheese. Sprinkle water over mixture gradually; shape into a ball. Roll pastry into 15" circle on floured surface. Place on baking sheet; turn up ¼" rim.

Combine creamer, brown sugar, sugar, ⅓ c. flour, ¼ tsp. salt, cinnamon and nutmeg. Sprinkle half of this mixture over pastry. Cut butter into remaining mixture until crumbly; set aside.

Arrange apple slices in circles on crust, overlapping the slices. Sprinkle with lemon juice and crumb mixture.

Bake in 450° oven 30 minutes or until apples are tender. Serve warm. Makes 12 servings.

BLUSHING APPLE DESSERT

⅓ c. butter	6 c. sliced, peeled apples
1 c. sifted flour	1 (3 oz.) pkg. strawberry
1 tblsp. sugar	flavored gelatin
¾ tsp. baking powder	2 tblsp. sugar
¼ tsp. salt	1 c. sifted flour
1 egg, beaten	1 c. sugar
1 tblsp. milk	½ c. butter

Cream butter until fluffy. Sift together 1 c. flour, 1 tblsp. sugar, baking powder and salt. Combine egg and milk. Add dry ingredients alternately with egg mixture; mix well. Press into 9" spring-form pan. Lay apple slices on dough so they overlap. Combine gelatin and 2 tblsp. sugar; sprinkle over apples.

Combine 1 c. flour and 1 c. sugar. Cut in ½ c. butter until coarse crumbs are formed. Sprinkle crumbs over apples.

Bake in 350° oven 50-60 minutes or until done. Serve with whipped cream, if desired. Makes 12 servings.

FROZEN APPLE CREAM

1 c. heavy cream	⅛ tsp. salt
¼ c. sugar	¾ c. grated, unpeeled
1½ tblsp. lemon juice	apples

Whip cream until stiff. Fold in sugar, lemon juice, salt and apples. Pour into 9×5×3″ loaf pan. Cover with aluminum foil. Freeze until solid. Spoon into sherbet glasses to serve. Makes 6 servings.

APPLE ICE CREAM SUNDAES

Red cinnamon candies   **Vanilla ice cream**
Applesauce

Dissolve a few cinnamon candies in warm applesauce. Spoon over scoops of vanilla ice cream.
Variation: Serve warm applesauce over cinnamon ice cream.

APPLE DUMPLINGS

2 c. sifted flour	Sugar
1 tsp. salt	Ground cinnamon
2 tsp. baking powder	2 c. sugar
¾ c. shortening	¼ tsp. ground cinnamon
3 tblsp. milk	¼ tsp. ground nutmeg
8 medium apples, peeled	2 c. hot water
and cored	¼ c. butter

Sift together flour, salt and baking powder. Cut in shortening until crumbly. Add milk; stir until mixture forms a ball.

Divide dough in half. Roll out on floured surface to 12″ square. Cut in 4 (6″) squares. Place 1 apple in the center of each square. Sprinkle each with sugar and cinnamon. Brings corners of dough to top of apple. Pinch edges together. Place in buttered 13×9×2″ baking dish. Repeat with remaining dough.

Combine 2 c. sugar, ¼ tsp. cinnamon and nutmeg in saucepan. Add water and butter. Stir over medium heat until sugar is dissolved and butter is melted. Pour syrup around apple dumplings.

Bake in 350° oven 50-60 minutes or until apples are tender. Serve warm with cream, if you wish. Makes 8 servings.

QUICK CARAMEL APPLES

6 to 8 wooden skewers
6 to 8 medium apples

1 (14 oz.) pkg. caramels
3 tblsp. water

Insert skewers in apples. Melt caramels in top of double boiler over simmering water. Add water slowly, blending until smooth. Leaving caramel mixture over hot water, dip apples into caramel mixture. Twirl apples so all sides are covered. Place on waxed paper to cool. (Store in refrigerator if weather is humid.) Makes 6 to 8 servings.

APPLE MACAROON DESSERT

4 c. sliced, peeled apples
½ c. sugar
½ tsp. ground cinnamon
½ c. chopped pecans
½ c. coconut
½ c. butter

½ c. sugar
1 egg, beaten
¾ c. sifted flour
½ tsp. vanilla
Sweetened whipped
  cream

Arrange apples in 9″ pie plate. Combine ½ c. sugar and cinnamon; sprinkle over apples. Top with pecans and coconut.

Cream butter until fluffy. Gradually beat in ½ c. sugar. Add egg, flour and vanilla; mix well. Spread over apple mixture.

Bake in 350° oven 30-35 minutes or until top is

golden brown. Serve warm or cold with whipped cream. Makes 8 servings.

BUTTERSCOTCH APPLE DESSERT

---

2 eggs
1½ c. sugar
3 c. sliced, peeled apples
1½ c. sifted flour
1½ tsp. baking soda
¾ tsp. ground nutmeg
¾ tsp. ground cinnamon
1 tsp. salt

1 c. chopped nuts
2 tblsp. flour
¾ c. sugar
¾ c. brown sugar, firmly
    packed
¾ c. light cream
⅓ c. butter

Beat eggs well. Add 1½ c. sugar gradually and beat until thick and lemon-colored. Fold in apple slices.

Sift together 1½ c. flour, baking soda, nutmeg, cinnamon and salt. Fold into egg mixture with nuts. Pour batter in greased 13 × 9 × 2″ baking pan.

Bake in 325° oven 50-60 minutes or until done. Serve warm with butterscotch sauce.

Combine 2 tblsp. flour, ¾ c. sugar and brown sugar in top of double boiler. Stir in cream and butter. Cook over simmering water, stirring occasionally, until thickened. Makes 16 servings.

APPLESAUCE WHIP

1 c. sweetened apple-
   sauce
1 tsp. red cinnamon
   candies

1 egg white, beaten
   until stiff

Combine applesauce with cinnamon candies. Fold in egg white. Chill in refrigerator. Spoon into serving dishes. Makes 4 servings.

APPLE GRAHAM CRACKER DELIGHT

16 graham crackers
Applesauce

Whipped cream

Use 4 graham crackers for each serving. Spread a generous amount of applesauce on 3 of the crackers. Stack them like a layer cake. Frost outside of stack with whipped cream. Chill at least 20 minutes. Makes 4 servings.

Pies and Pastries

PASTRY FOR 2-CRUST 9" PIE

2 c. sifted flour	¾ c. shortening
1 tsp. salt	4 to 6 tblsp. water

Combine flour and salt in bowl. Cut in shortening until particles are size of peas. Sprinkle mixture with water, a tablespoon at a time, tossing together with fork until flour is moistened. Form into a ball.

Divide in half. Roll out one half on floured surface to fit 9" pie pan. Roll out remaining dough for top crust. Cut several vents in top. Makes enough pastry for 2-crust 9" pie.

OLD-FASHIONED APPLE PIE

Pastry for 2-crust 9" pie	¾ c. sugar
6 c. sliced, peeled apples	¼ tsp. ground cinnamon
	2 tblsp. butter

Combine apples, sugar and cinnamon; mix well. Turn into pastry-lined pie pan. Dot with butter: Cover with top crust; cut vents. Flute edges.

Bake in 400° oven 45-50 minutes or until crust is golden brown and apples are tender. Makes 6 to 8 servings.

APPLE BLUEBERRY PIE

Unbaked 8″ pie shell
3 c. sliced, peeled
  apples
1 c. blueberries, fresh
  or frozen and thawed

1 c. sugar
1½ tblsp. cornstarch
½ tsp. ground cinnamon
Cheese Crumb Topping
  (recipe follows)

Combine apples, blueberries, sugar, cornstarch and cinnamon; mix well. Turn into pie shell.

Combine Cheese Crumb Topping. Sprinkle over apple mixture.

Bake in 425° oven 40-50 minutes or until apples are tender. Makes 6 servings.

Cheese Crumb Topping: Combine 1 c. sifted flour, 2 tblsp. sugar, 3 tblsp. butter and ½ c. shredded Cheddar cheese. Mix until crumbly.

APPLE CRANBERRY RELISH PIE

Unbaked 9″ pie shell
6 c. sliced, peeled
  apples
⅓ c. cranberry relish,
  canned or frozen

¾ c. sugar
1½ tblsp. cornstarch
⅛ tsp. ground cinnamon

Combine apples, cranberry relish, sugar, cornstarch and cinnamon. Turn into pie shell.

Bake in 400° oven 45 minutes or until apples are tender. Makes 6 to 8 servings.

UPSIDE DOWN APPLE PECAN PIE

Pastry for 2-crust 9″ pie
¼ c. soft butter
⅓ c. pecan halves
⅔ c. brown sugar,
   firmly packed
6 c. sliced, peeled
   apples

1 tblsp. lemon juice
1 tblsp. flour
½ c. sugar
½ tsp. ground cinnamon
¼ tsp. salt

Spread butter evenly on bottom and sides of 9″ pie pan. Press pecan halves, rounded side down, into butter. Sprinkle brown sugar evenly over pecans.

Roll out ½ of pastry. Place over mixture in pan, trimming edges evenly.

Combine apples, lemon juice, flour, sugar, cinnamon and salt. Arrange in crust. Top with remaining pastry. Flute edges and cut vents in top.

Bake in 350° oven 1 hour or until apples are tender. Remove from oven when syrup stops bubbling. Place serving plate over pie and invert. Remove pie pan. Makes 6 to 8 servings.

APPLE CREAM PIE

Quick Pastry (recipe
    follows)
2½ c. sliced, peeled
    apples
½ c. sugar

¼ c. flour
⅛ tsp. ground nutmeg
1 c. heavy cream

Prepare Quick Pastry.

Combine apples, sugar, flour and nutmeg. Turn into pastry-lined pie pan.

Bake in 375° oven 10 minutes. Pour cream over all. Bake 30-35 minutes or until apples are tender. Makes 6 to 8 servings.

Quick Pastry: Sift together 1½ c. sifted flour, 2 tblsp. sugar and ⅛ tsp. salt. Cut in ½ c. butter until crumbly. Combine 3 egg yolks and 1 tblsp. water. Add to crumb mixture; mix well. Knead until smooth. Pat into 9″ pie pan with fingers. Flute edges.

GOURMET APPLE PIE

Unbaked 9" pie shell	**1 egg yolk, beaten**
1 tblsp. dry bread	**1 c. heavy cream**
crumbs	**½ c. sugar**
1 tblsp. chopped toasted	**¼ tsp. ground cinnamon**
almonds	**⅛ tsp. ground nutmeg**
5 c. sliced, peeled	**1½ tblsp. melted butter**
apples	**3 tblsp. sugar**
1 egg, beaten	

Sprinkle bread crumbs and almonds in pie shell. Arrange apples in pie shell.

Bake in 350° oven 5 minutes.

Combine 1 egg, 1 egg yolk, heavy cream, ½ c. sugar, cinnamon and nutmeg; blend well. Pour ½ of cream mixture over apples. Continue baking for 30 minutes or until custard is firm. Pour remaining cream mixture evenly over all. Bake 30 more minutes or until a knife inserted near the edge comes out clean. Remove from oven. Pour butter over the top. Sprinkle with 3 tblsp. sugar. Return to oven long enough to glaze topping, about 8 minutes. Cool before cutting. Makes 6 to 8 servings.

SOUR CREAM APPLE PIE

Unbaked 9″ pie shell	**1 tsp. vanilla**
2 tblsp. flour	**¼ tsp. ground nutmeg**
⅛ tsp. salt	**2 c. sliced, peeled**
¾ c. sugar	**apples**
1 egg	**Nut Topping (recipe**
1 c. dairy sour cream	**follows)**

Combine flour, salt, sugar, egg, sour cream, vanilla and nutmeg; beat well. Stir in apples. Pour into pie shell.

Bake in 400° oven 15 minutes. Reduce oven to 350° and bake 30 minutes longer. Remove from oven; sprinkle with Nut Topping. Return to oven 10 minutes or until lightly browned. Makes 6 to 8 servings.

Nut Topping: Combine ¼ c. sugar, ¼ c. flour, ¾ tsp. ground cinnamon, ¼ c. chopped nuts and ¼ c. butter; mix until crumbly.

GLOSSY APPLE RAISIN PIE

Pastry for 2-crust 9" pie
6 c. sliced, peeled apples
¾ c. sugar
2 tblsp. flour
½ tsp. ground cinnamon

¼ tsp. salt
½ c. raisins
2 tblsp. orange juice
¼ c. butter
Orange Glaze (recipe follows)

Combine apples, sugar, flour, cinnamon, salt and raisins; mix well. Turn into pastry-lined pie pan. Sprinkle with orange juice; dot with butter. Place top crust over filling. Cut vents; flute edges.

Bake in 400° oven 40 minutes or until apples are tender. Spread Orange Glaze over hot pie. Makes 6 to 8 servings.

Orange Glaze: Combine 1 c. sifted confectioners sugar, 3 tblsp. orange juice and 1 tsp. grated orange peel; mix until smooth.

APPLE CRUMB PIE WITH YOGURT

Unbaked 9″ pie shell
¾ c. sugar
¼ c. brown sugar, firmly packed
2 tblsp. flour
½ tsp. ground cinnamon
¼ tsp. ground nutmeg
1 tsp. lemon juice
¾ c. plain or vanilla yogurt
6 c. sliced, peeled apples
½ c. flour
½ c. brown sugar, firmly packed
¼ c. butter

Combine sugar, ¼ c. brown sugar, 2 tblsp. flour, cinnamon, nutmeg, lemon juice and yogurt; blend well. Stir in apples. Turn into pie shell.

Combine ½ c. flour and ½ c. brown sugar. Cut in butter until crumbly. Sprinkle over apple mixture.

Bake in 350° oven 50 minutes or until apples are tender. Makes 6 to 8 servings.

APPLE PUMPKIN PIE

Pastry for two 8" pie
  shells
4 c. sliced, peeled
  apples
⅔ c. sugar
3 tblsp. flour
2 c. canned pumpkin
½ c. sugar
½ c. brown sugar, firmly
  packed

¼ tsp. ground cloves
1 tsp. ground cinnamon
½ tsp. ground nutmeg
¼ tsp. ground ginger
2 eggs, beaten
1½ c. evaporated milk
1 tblsp. butter

Combine apples, sugar and flour; mix well. Combine pumpkin, ½ c. sugar, brown sugar, cloves, cinnamon, nutmeg, ginger and eggs; blend well. Heat evaporated milk and butter until butter is melted. Add to pumpkin mixture; blend well. Stir in apple mixture. Pour mixture into pie shells.

Bake in 425° oven 10 minutes. Reduce temperature to 350° and continue baking 40 minutes or until knife inserted at edge of filling comes out clean. Makes 12 servings.

CRANBERRY APPLE PIE

Orange Pastry (recipe
  follows)
1 c. cranberries
3 c. sliced, peeled
  apples

1 c. sugar
2 tblsp. flour
⅛ tsp. salt
2 tblsp. butter

Prepare Orange Pastry.

Combine cranberries, apples, sugar, flour and salt; mix well. Turn into pastry-lined pie pan. Cover with top crust. Cut vents in top. Flute edges.

Bake in 400° oven 50 minutes or until apples are tender. Makes 6 to 8 servings.

Orange Pastry: Sift together 2 c. sifted flour and 1 tsp. salt. Cut in ⅔ c. shortening until crumbly. Add 1 tsp. grated orange peel and ⅓ c. orange juice. Toss together with fork until flour is moistened. Form into a ball. Divide in half. Roll out one half on floured surface to fit 9″ pie pan.

APPLE PEAR CRUMB PIE

Unbaked 9″ pie shell	**¼ tsp. salt**
2 c. diced, peeled	**¼ tsp. ground cinnamon**
apples	**½ c. raisins**
3½ c. canned pears,	**1 tblsp. lemon juice**
drained and sliced	**2 tblsp. butter**
⅓ c. sugar	**Crumb Topping (recipe**
2 tblsp. flour	**follows)**

Combine apples, pears, sugar, flour, salt, cinnamon, raisins and lemon juice; mix well. Turn into pie shell. Dot with butter. Sprinkle with Crumb Topping.

Bake in 450° oven 10 minutes. Cover with aluminum foil and continue baking at 350° 40 minutes or until apples are tender. Serve warm. Makes 6 to 8 servings.

Crumb Topping: Combine ¼ c. flour, ½ c. brown sugar and ¼ tsp. salt. Cut in 1 (3 oz.) pkg. cream cheese until crumbly. Stir in ½ c. chopped walnuts.

FRENCH APPLE PIE

Unbaked 9″ pie shell
7c. sliced, peeled
   apples
⅔ c. sugar

½ tsp. ground cinnamon
1½ tblsp. butter
Topping (recipe follows)

Combine apples, sugar and cinnamon; mix well. Turn into pie shell. Dot with butter. Sprinkle with Topping.

Bake in 400° oven 50 minutes or until apples are tender. Serve warm. Makes 6 to 8 servings.

Topping: Combine 1 c. flour, ½ c. brown sugar, firmly packed, and ¼ tsp. ground cinnamon. Cut in ½ c. butter until crumbly.

APPLE ICE CREAM PIE

Baked 9″ pie shell
¾ c. apple juice
1 (3 oz.) pkg. lemon
   flavored gelatin

1 pt. vanilla ice cream
1½ c. applesauce

Bring apple juice to a boil. Remove from heat and stir in gelatin. Stir until dissolved. Add ice cream and stir until melted. Blend in applesauce. Chill until mixture begins to thicken. Turn into pie shell. Chill until set. Makes 6 to 8 servings.

Preserves

SMOOTH APPLESAUCE

4 medium apples   **¼ c. sugar**
½ c. water

Quarter and core apples. Place apples and water in saucepan. Cover and simmer 10 minutes or until apples are tender. Put apples through a food mill. Stir in sugar. Makes about 2 cups.

(You'll save time if you don't peel the apples; the food mill strains out the peel after cooking. But if you wish, you can peel them and strain to make a very smooth sauce.)

Variations:
Chunky Applesauce: Peel apples and cook as above. Break up cooked apples slightly with a fork.
Large Quantity: Quarter and core apples. Place in a large kettle with enough water so fruit will not stick to bottom during cooking. Cover and simmer 10 minutes or until apples are tender. Put through food mill. (4 lbs. apples yields 1½ qts. applesauce.)
Applesauce Tricks: Stir cinnamon candies into applesauce. Serve hot or cold with pork.

Mix a little horseradish with applesauce. Good with ham, beef or pork.

Flavor applesauce with mint and tint a pale green with food color. Serve with lamb.

APPLE BUTTER

6 lbs. apples, quartered and cored	3 c. sugar
	1½ tsp. ground cinnamon
2 qts. apple juice	½ tsp. ground cloves

Combine apples and apple juice in saucepan. Cook until apples are tender. Put through a food mill. Place 12 c. apple pulp into kettle. Cook pulp until thick enough to round up in spoon. Stir pulp frequently as it thickens to prevent sticking. Add sugar, cinnamon and cloves; continue cooking slowly until mixture is thick, about 1 hour. Pour into hot, sterilized jars to within ¼ inch from top. Adjust jar lids. Process in boiling water bath 10 minutes.

APPLE JELLY

3 lbs. tart apples	2 tblsp. lemon juice
3 c. water	3 c. sugar

Choose tart apples, ¾ of them fully ripe and ¼ under-ripe. Wash, remove stem and blossom ends. Do not peel or core. Cut apples into small pieces. Place apples and water in saucepan. Cover and bring to a boil over high heat. Reduce heat and simmer 20-25 minutes or until apples are soft.

Place fruit in colander lined with cheesecloth or dampened jelly bag. Let fruit drip through without pressing so jelly will be clear. However, you will get more juice by pressing and/or twisting bag or using a fruit press.

Measure apple juice into kettle. Add lemon juice and sugar. Stir well. Bring to a boil over high heat until temperature is 120° or jelly mixture sheets from spoon. Remove from heat. Skim off foam quickly. Pour jelly immediately into hot, sterilized jars. Cover with ⅛ inch melted paraffin. Makes about 5 (6 oz.) jars.

Variation:
Crabapple Jelly: Use 3 lbs. crabapples and 3 c. water to make 4 c. juice. Omit lemon juice. Follow directions for making Apple Jelly.

APPLE CONSERVE

4½ c. finely chopped, unpeeled tart apples	1 pkg. powdered fruit pectin
½ c. water	5 c. sugar
¼ c. lemon juice	½ c. chopped walnuts
½ c. raisins	

Combine apples, water, lemon juice and raisins in kettle. Add fruit pectin; stir well. Place over high heat and bring to a full boil. Stirring constantly, stir in sugar. Bring to a full boil again. Boil 1 minute, stirring constantly. Stir in nuts. Remove from heat. Skim and stir 5 minutes. Ladle into hot, sterilized jars to within ½ inch from top. Adjust jar lids. Process in boiling water bath 10 minutes. Makes 5 half-pints.

CRABAPPLE PICKLES

3 qts. crabapples	2 c. water
2 c. vinegar	2 sticks cinnamon
4 c. sugar	1 tsp. whole cloves

Wash crabapples using only ones free from blemishes. Combine vinegar, sugar and water in kettle. Bring to a boil. Tie cinnamon and cloves in cheesecloth; add to mixture. Boil 10 minutes. Add crabapples to syrup. Cook until almost tender. Place crabapples in hot, sterilized jars. Pour hot syrup over crabapples to with ½ inch from top. Adjust jar lids. Process in boiling hot water bath 10 minutes. Makes 6 pints.

ESTHER'S APPLE CHUTNEY

4 c. chopped, peeled apples	¼ c. vinegar
½ c. water	1 tsp. ground cinnamon
3 c. sugar	¼ tsp. ground cloves
	¼ tsp. salt

Place apples and water in 2-qt. saucepan. Bring to a boil. Cover and simmer 10 minutes or until apples are tender. Stir in sugar, vinegar, cinnamon and cloves. Simmer, uncovered, 50 minutes or until mixture thickens. Pour into hot, sterilized jars to within ½ inch from top. Adjust jar lids. Process in boiling water bath 10 minutes. Makes 4 half-pints.

Salads

WALDORF SALAD

2 c. diced, unpeeled
  apples
½ tsp. lemon juice
⅛ tsp. salt

1 c. chopped celery
½ c. chopped walnuts
¼ c. mayonnaise
Salad greens

Combine apples, lemon juice, salt, celery and walnuts. Fold in mayonnaise. Chill. Serve on salad greens. Makes 6 servings.

TUNA APPLE SALAD

1 (12 oz.) can tuna,
  drained and flaked
1½ c. diced, unpeeled
  apples
½ c. celery

½ c. chopped walnuts
Mayonnaise or salad
  dressing
Lettuce

Combine tuna, apples, celery and walnuts. Add enough mayonnaise to moisten. Chill. Serve in lettuce cups. Makes 4 to 6 servings.

FESTIVE RED AND WHITE SALAD

½ c. red cinnamon
  candies
1 (3 oz.) pkg. lemon
  flavor gelatin
1 c. boiling water
1½ c. sweetened apple
  sauce

1 (8 oz.) pkg. cream
  cheese, softened
½ c. chopped nuts
½ c. chopped celery
½ c. mayonnaise

Dissolve cinnamon candies and gelatin in boiling water. Add applesauce; mix well. Pour half of mixture in 8″ square baking pan. Chill until firm. Let remaining gelatin mixture stand at room temperature.

Stir cream cheese until smooth. Add nuts and celery; mix well. Stir in mayonnnaise. Spread over chilled gelatin layer. Pour remaining gelatin mixture evenly on top. Chill until firm. Cut in squares. Makes 6 servings.

GOLDEN SALAD

2 c. shredded carrots
1 c. diced, unpeeled
  apples

½ c. raisins
1 tsp. lemon juice
Salad dressing

Combine carrots, apples, raisins and lemon juice. Add enough salad dressing to moisten. Chill. Makes 4 to 5 servings.

BLUSHING APPLE FRUIT SALAD

2 c. whole cranberries
⅓ c. sugar
2 c. diced, peeled
   apples

½ c. canned crushed
   pineapple, drained
½ c. miniature marsh-
   mallows
½ c. heavy cream, whipped

Put cranberries through food grinder. Sprinkle with sugar. Let stand 2 hours. Drain.

Combine drained cranberries, apples, pineapple and marshmallows. Chill. Just before serving, fold in whipped cream. Makes 6 to 8 servings.

CINNAMON APPLE SALAD

½ c. red cinnamon
   candies
½ c. sugar
2 c. water

6 medium apples,
   pared and cored
Cottage cheese

Combine cinnamon candies, sugar and water in 2-qt. saucepan. Bring to a boil, stirring constantly. Add apples and simmer, turning occasionally until tender. Remove apples; place in glass dish. Continue cooking sugar mixture until thick and syrupy. Remove from heat and pour over apples. Chill. Stuff cavity of apples with cottage cheese. Serve on lettuce. Makes 6 servings.

APPLE CHEESE SALAD

2 c. diced, unpeeled
  apples
1 c. sliced celery
¾ c. canned pineapple
  tidbits, drained

½ c. cubed Cheddar
  cheese
½ c. salad dressing or
  mayonnaise
Lettuce

Combine apples, celery, pineapple, cheese and salad dressing; toss well. Serve on lettuce. Makes 4 to 6 servings.

CHAPTER VII

Fun with Apples

Every kid bobs for apples at Hallowe'en, but have you ever run an apple race? Or tried making apple head dolls? Or apple candle holders? Or pomanders, for gifts or to perfume your own closets? Here are suggestions for several ways to have fun with apples.

Pomander Balls. Originally, pomanders were apple-shaped mixtures of aromatic substances, which people carried as protection against infection. Now, we enjoy them for the pleasant way they scent our closets.

For each ball, you need an apple, a box of whole cloves, a pipe cleaner and ribbon. Poke holes all over the apple with a sharp-pointed round toothpick and insert cloves. Cloves should be close together, completely covering the apple. Insert a pipe cleaner into the stem end—be sure it's secure. Bend it to make a hanger, and decorate with a ribbon bow. The apple will dry, but the spicy fragrance will remain.

Apple Centerpiece. Select the reddest, most attractive apples you can find. Wash and polish them until they shine. Pile them on a tray with sprigs of evergreen. For a Christmas table, set some miniature Santa figures climbing over the greens—or the Scandinavian *nisse* or *tomte*. For an autumn table, use yellow apples like Golden Delicious or Honey Gold, and arrange some of fall's bright colored leaves among the greens.

Apple Candle Holders. Select firm, well-shaped red apples. Polish highly. Remove the core from the stem end with an apple corer, leaving about ½ inch of fruit at the base. Insert candles.

Party Favors. Use apples as flag holders. For an international party, put an apple with the flag of a different nation at each place at the table. If you're entertaining after a football game, make college banners of construction paper in the appropriate colors. Glue them to thin wood picks and insert in apples.

Santa Claus Favors. For each apple Santa, you'll need a large red apple, 5 large marshmallows, 6 large round red gumdrops, 4 whole cloves, 3 cinnamon candies (red hots) and round toothpicks. Make legs and arms by threading a marshmallow and a gumdrop on a toothpick; insert in apple with gumdrop next to apple (marshmallow makes "fur" cuffs). Make the head the same way, adding a gumdrop hat. Press red hots into marshmallow head for eyes and nose. Stick cloves into apple body for buttons. If you wish, add beard and pompom of cotton.

Bobbing for Apples. Here's the favorite game for Hallowe'en parties. To play it, fill a washtub, baby's bathtub or large plastic vessel three-quarters full of water. Count a few more apples than there are players. Float the apples in the water. The idea is for players to catch an apple with their teeth—without using hands—and within a certain time limit. The person who gets his apple out of the water first is the winner, but others continue to try until time is called.

Apple on a String. Another favorite Hallowe'en contest. Each player—with his hands behind him—tries to eat an apple dangling from a string in a doorway or some open place. To make the game more interesting, hang the apples at different heights.

Apple Peel Fortunes. Write out fortunes that will be appropriate for the guests you've invited. Turn them over and number the other side; arrange them, number-side-up, on the floor. Ask each guest to peel an apple and toss the peeling over his or her shoulder. The fortune nearest where the peeling falls will be his to read aloud.

Apple Puppet Contest. Divide the group into teams. Give each team several apples, an apple corer, knife, and pins, and have available a large box of articles that can be used for clothing the puppets—scarves, doll hats and dresses, ribbons, feathers, jewelry, etc. Each team decides on a fairy tale or Mother Goose rhyme to enact. Players then carve appropriate apple puppets, coring the apples to fit players' index fingers. Puppet faces are carved much like a jack-o'-lantern, and painted, if desired, with lipstick or crayons. Stage can be a table covered with a cloth to hide the puppeteers.

Apple Race. This game can be very funny. Divide the group into teams. Give each player a toothpick. Object is to push an apple along from starting point to goal using only the toothpick held in the mouth—no hands. The side that gets all its apples to the goal first wins.

Apple Seed Guessing Game. Show guests a shiny red apple and ask each one to write down the number of seeds in the apple. Collect the answers; then cut the apple and let everyone help count seeds. Give a prize to the person whose guess is closest.

Make a Character Doll

Whenever a rag doll needed a new head, the pioneer mother or father simply carved one from an apple and set it in the sun to dry. Mother pinched it now and then to shape the nose, eyes and chin.

This old craft is being revived today, an inexpensive and absorbing project for you to try. As the apple dries out, you see the face you carved in it shrivel and become wrinkled. In a few weeks, the apple head will be weathered looking, creased with the furrows of old age. Once dry, apple heads last indefinitely. When the dolls are dressed in character—as grandmothers, grandfathers, or figures from history—they make a fascinating display.

To carve apple heads, pare a firm, juicy apple as thinly as possible. Remove the stem and blossom end, and core the fruit or not, as you please. With the tip of a small, sharp knife, carve features fairly large (see Figure 1). Use a light touch, and allow for shrinkage. Cut slits for eyes about ⅓ of the way down from the stem end and press in a piece of peeling above the eyes to make brows. Press with thumb to deepen eye sockets. Carve nose carefully, making sure it protrudes. Pinch nose and chin to form the shape you want. Carve

Figure 1

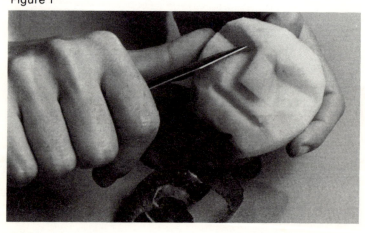

ears. Cut a slit for the mouth; if you wish, press in a bit of peel. For eyes, insert apple or other dark seeds, black beads or whole cloves into sockets. For rosy cheeks, rub with lipstick or paint with water colors.

You can air dry apple heads. Skewer them on pointed sticks and set each stick in a glass, so air can circulate all around the apples. This will take about three weeks. To hurry the process, begin drying in the oven. Place apple heads on a cookie sheet and put them in a 150°-200° F. oven for a few hours. (If you have a gas oven

Figure 2

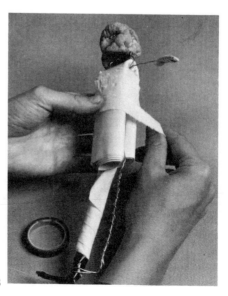

Figure 3

with pilot light which keeps the oven warm, simply leave them in it overnight.)

If you cored the apples, stuff the hollows with cotton and glue when you take them out of the oven. Hang each apple head up to finish drying in a spot where air circulation is good. As they dry, pinch them to develop the features and expressions you want. Drying time will depend on how humid it is. If they feel sticky after a week, let them dry a few days longer. Apples will shrink to about ⅓ their original size; they will be slightly spongy, but not hard.

Make body frames from easily bent wire (18 or 20 gauge). Insert two pieces 10-12 inches long into the blossom end of the apple, about an inch apart, for body and legs. Cut a piece 8-10 inches long for arms and place it at chest height. Fasten arms to body and reinforce shoulders by twisting in another short piece of wire (see Figure 2). Double back ends of wire to make hands and feet; cover with tape. Stuff the body with old nylon hose, cotton or folded paper, and wrap with narrow strips of sheeting (see Figure 3).

Use cotton, fiber-fill, white lamb's wool or steel wool for wigs and chin whiskers. Look through illustrated history books, story books or your own family picture albums to get ideas for dressing the dolls.

Photos: Iowa State University

Index